AA

Qualificati

AQ2013

LEVEL 3

(QCF)

QUESTIO

2015 Edition

For assessments from September 2015

633310

Third edition June 2015
ISBN 9781 4727 2201 0

Previous edition June 2014
ISBN 9781 4727 0935 6

British Library Cataloguing-in-Publication Data
A catalogue record for this book is available from the British Library

Published by
BPP Learning Media Ltd
BPP House
Aldine Place
London W12 8AA

www.bpp.com/learningmedia

Printed in the United Kingdom by Martins of Berwick
Sea View Works
Spittal
Berwick-Upon-Tweed
TD15 1RS

Your learning materials, published by BPP Learning Media Ltd, are
printed on paper sourced from traceable sustainable sources.

We are grateful to the AAT for permission to reproduce the AAT
sample assessment(s). The answers to the AAT sample assessment(s)
have been published by the AAT. All other answers have been
prepared by BPP Learning Media Ltd.

CONTENTS

A NOTE ABOUT COPYRIGHT

INTRODUCTION

This is BPP Learning Media's AAT Question Bank for Prepare Final Accounts for Sole Traders and Partnerships. It is part of a suite of ground breaking resources produced by BPP Learning Media for the AAT's assessments under the Qualification and Credit Cramework (QCF).

The Prepare Final Accounts for Sole Traders and Partnerships assessment will be **computer assessed**. As well as being available in the traditional paper format, this **Question Bank is available in an online format** containing tasks similar to those you will encounter in the AAT's testing environment. BPP Learning Media believe that the best way to practise for an online assessment is in an online environment. However, if you are unable to practise in the online environment you will find that all tasks in the paper question bank have been written in a style that is as close as possible to the style that you will be presented with in your online assessment.

This Question Bank has been written in conjunction with the BPP Text, and has been carefully designed to enable students to practise all of the learning outcomes and assessment criteria for the units that make up Prepare Final Accounts for Sole Traders and Partnerships. It is fully up to date as at June 2015 and reflects both the AAT's unit guide and the sample assessments provided by the AAT.

This Question Bank contains these key features:

- Tasks corresponding to each chapter of the Text. Some tasks are designed for learning purposes, others are of assessment standard

- The AAT's AQ2013 sample assessments and answers for Prepare Final Accounts for Sole Traders and Partnerships

The emphasis in all tasks and assessments is on the practical application of the skills acquired.

VAT

You will find tasks throughout this question bank which need you to calculate or be aware of a rate of VAT. This is stated at 20% in these examples and questions.

Approaching the assessment

When you sit the assessment it is very important that you follow the on screen instructions. This means you need to carefully read the instructions, both on the introduction screens and during specific tasks.

When you access the assessment you should be presented with an introductory screen with information similar to that shown below (taken from the introductory screen from one of the AAT's AQ2013 sample assessments for Prepare Final Accounts for Sole Traders and Partnerships).

We have provided the following assessment to help you familiarise yourself with AAT's e-assessment environment. It is designed to demonstrate as many as possible of the question types you may find in a live assessment. It is not designed to be used on its own to determine whether you are ready for a live assessment.

Each task is independent. You will not need to refer to your answers to previous tasks.
Read every task carefully to make sure you understand what is required.

Where the date is relevant, it is given in the task data.

Both minus signs and brackets can be used to indicate negative numbers UNLESS task instructions say otherwise.

The standard rate of VAT is 20%.

You must use a full stop to indicate a decimal point.
For example, write 100.57 NOT 100,57 or 100 57

You may use a comma to indicate a number in the thousands, but you don't have to.
For example, 10000 and 10,000 are both OK.

Other indicators are not compatible with the computer-marked system.

Complete all 5 tasks.

The actual instructions will vary depending on the subject you are studying for. It is very important you read the instructions on the introductory screen and apply them in the assessment. You don't want to lose marks when you know the correct answer just because you have not entered it in the right format.

In general, the rules set out in the AAT sample assessments for the subject you are studying for will apply in the real assessment, but you should again read the information on this screen in the real assessment carefully just to make sure. This screen may also confirm the VAT rate used if applicable.

A full stop is needed to indicate a decimal point. We would recommend using minus signs to indicate negative numbers and leaving out the comma signs to indicate thousands, as this results in a lower number of key strokes and less margin for error when working under time pressure. Having said that, you can use whatever is easiest for you as long as you operate within the rules set out for your particular assessment.

You have to show competence throughout the assessment and you should therefore complete all of the tasks. Don't leave questions unanswered.

In some assessments written or complex tasks may be human marked. In this case you are given a blank space or table to enter your answer into. You are told in the practice assessments which tasks these are (note: there may be none if all answers are marked by the computer).

If these involve calculations, it is a good idea to decide in advance how you are going to lay out your answers to such tasks by practising answering them on a word document, and certainly you should try all such tasks in this Question Bank and in the AAT's environment using the sample/practice assessments.

When asked to fill in tables, or gaps, never leave any blank even if you are unsure of the answer. Fill in your best estimate.

Note that for some assessments where there is a lot of scenario information or tables of data provided (eg tax tables), you may need to access these via 'pop-ups'. Instructions will be provided on how you can bring up the necessary data during the assessment.

Finally, take note of any task specific instructions once you are in the assessment. For example you may be asked to enter a date in a certain format or to enter a number to a certain number of decimal places.

Remember you can practise the BPP questions in this Question Bank in an online environment on our dedicated AAT Online page. On the same page is a link to the current AAT Sample Assessments as well.

If you have any comments about this book, please email nisarahmed@bpp.com or write to Nisar Ahmed, AAT Head of Programme, BPP Learning Media Ltd, BPP House, Aldine Place, London W12 8AA.

Question bank

Chapter 1 – Introduction to financial statements

Task 1.1

Indicate whether each of the following balances is an asset, a liability, income, an expense or capital.

Balance	Asset ✓	Liability ✓	Income ✓	Expense ✓	Capital ✓
Salaries				✓	
Bank overdraft		✓			
Office costs				✓	
Bank loan		✓			
Capital					✓
Receivables			✓		
Purchases				✓	
Discount received			✓		

Task 1.2

Given below is a trial balance for a business. Indicate with a tick as to whether each item in the trial balance falls into the category of asset, liability, income, expense or capital.

Balance	Debit £	Credit £	Asset ✓	Liability ✓	Income ✓	Expense ✓	Capital ✓
Rent cost	11,400					✓	
Sales		143,000			✓		
Opening inventory	2,400		✓				
Payables		6,000		✓			
Purchases	86,200					✓	
Drawings	17,910						
Telephone costs	1,250					✓	
Discounts received		80			✓		
Distribution costs	400					✓	
Motor vehicles	32,600		✓				
Receivables	11,900		✓				
Discounts allowed	120					✓	
Capital		40,000					✓
Wages	20,600					✓	
Heat and light	1,600					✓	
Computer	2,400		✓				
Bank	300			✓			
	189,080	189,080					

Task 1.3

A business has made sales during the year of £867,450. The opening inventory of goods was £24,578 and the closing inventory was £30,574. During the year there were purchases made of £426,489. Distribution costs for the year were £104,366 and administration expenses totalled £87,689.

What are the gross profit and profit for the year?

Gross profit	£	1287943
Profit for the year	£	1095888

Task 1.4

What are the main categories of items that appear on a statement of financial position for a business?

Assets   Liability

Task 1.5

Decide whether each of the following balances would be an asset or liability on the statement of financial position or an item of income or expense in profit or loss. For the statement of financial position items indicate what types of asset or liability they are.

Balance	Asset ✓	Liability ✓	Income ✓	Expense ✓	Type of asset/liability
A company car	✓				
Interest on a bank overdraft			✓		
A bank loan repayable in five years		✓			
Petty cash of £25			✓		
The portion of rent paid covering the period after the statement of financial position date				✓	
Freehold property	✓				
Payment of wages for a manager with a two year service contract				✓	
An irrecoverable debt written off				✓	

Task 1.6

Describe the form and function of the statement of financial position and the statement of profit or loss.

Statement of financial position (SFP)

Statement of profit or loss (P/L)

Task 1.7

Computer software, although for long-term use in the business, is charged to the statement of profit or loss when purchased as its value is small in comparison with the hardware.

Which accounting concept determines this treatment?

Task 1.8

Explain each of the following four objectives which determine an organisation's choice of accounting policies.

Relevance

Reliability

Comparability

Ease of understanding

Task 1.9

Classify the following items as long-term assets ('non-current assets'), short-term assets ('current assets') or liabilities.

Classification	Non-current assets ✓	Current assets ✓	Liabilities ✓
A PC used in the accounts department of a shop		✓	
A PC on sale in an office equipment shop	✓		
Wages due to be paid to staff at the end of the week			✓
A van for sale in a motor dealer's showroom	✓		
A delivery van used in a grocer's business	✓		
An amount owing to a bank for a loan for the acquisition of a van, to be repaid over 9 months			✓

Task 1.10

Fill in the missing words:

The trading account shows the ⎕⎕⎕⎕⎕⎕ profit for the period.

The bottom line of the statement of profit or loss shows the ⎕⎕⎕⎕⎕⎕.

Task 1.11

	Yes ✓	No ✓
Is a bank overdraft a current liability?		

Task 1.12

Which of the following is not an accounting concept?

✓	
	Prudence
	Consistency
	Depreciation
	Accruals

Chapter 2 – Financial statements for a sole trader

Task 2.1

A sole trader had a capital balance of £32,569 on 1 May 20X8. During the year ended 30 April 20X9 the business made a profit for the year of £67,458 and the owner withdrew cash totalling £35,480 and goods with a cost of £1,680.

What is the capital balance at 30 April 20X9?

£

Task 2.2

A sole trader took goods from his business with a cost of £560 for his own personal use.

What is the double entry for this transaction?

Debit	
Credit	

Task 2.3

The draft trial balance for a sole trader for the year ended 30 June is as follows:

	£
Machinery at cost	140,000
Motor vehicles at cost	68,000
Furniture and fittings at cost	23,000
Accumulated depreciation – machinery	64,500
Accumulated depreciation – motor vehicles	31,200
Accumulated depreciation – furniture and fittings	13,400

The depreciation charges for the year to 30 June have not yet been accounted for and the sole trader's depreciation policies are:

Machinery	20% on cost
Motor vehicles	35% diminishing balance
Furniture and fittings	20% diminishing balance

What is the total carrying amount of the non-current assets that will appear in the statement of financial position at 30 June?

£

Task 2.4

A sole trader has produced the following final trial balance:

Trial balance at 31 May 20X8

	Debit £	Credit £
Bank		1,650
Capital		74,000
Payables		40,800
Receivables	60,000	
Discounts allowed	2,950	
Discounts received		2,000
Drawings	30,000	
Furniture and fittings at cost	24,500	
Electricity	2,950	
Insurance	2,300	
Miscellaneous expenses	1,500	
Motor expenses	3,100	
Motor vehicles at cost	48,000	
Purchases	245,000	
Allowance for doubtful debts		1,200
Accumulated depreciation – furniture and fittings		8,550
– motor vehicles		29,800
Rent	3,400	
Sales		369,000
Opening inventory	41,000	
Telephone costs	1,950	
VAT		4,100
Wages	52,000	
Closing inventory	43,500	43,500
Depreciation expense – furniture and fittings	2,450	
Depreciation expense – motor vehicles	7,800	
Irrecoverable debts expense	1,700	
Accruals		1,000
Prepayments	1,500	
	575,600	575,600

Prepare the financial statements for the year ended 31 May 20X8.

Statement of profit or loss for the year ended 31 May 20X8

	£	£
Sales revenue		
Cost of goods sold		
Gross profit		
Total expenses		
Profit/(loss) for the year		

Statement of financial position as at 31 May 20X8

	Cost £	Depreciation £	Carrying amount £
Non-current assets			
Current assets			
Current liabilities			
Net current assets			
Net assets			
Financed by:			

Task 2.5

Given below is the final trial balance of a sole trader for his year ended 30 June 20X8.

Final trial balance as at 30 June 20X8

	£	£
Administration expenses	7,490	
Bank	2,940	
Capital		60,000
Payables		20,200
Receivables	14,000	
Discounts allowed	2,510	
Discounts received		2,550
Distribution costs	1,530	
Drawings	14,600	
Machinery at cost	58,400	
Motor vehicles at cost	22,100	
Office costs	1,570	
Cost of goods sold	118,400	
Allowance for doubtful debts		280
Accumulated depreciation		
– Machinery		35,040
– Motor vehicles		12,785
Sales		167,400
Selling expenses	6,140	
VAT		3,690
Wages	16,700	
Closing inventory	18,200	
Irrecoverable debts expense	2,820	
Accruals		680
Prepayments	440	
Depreciation expense – machinery	11,680	
Depreciation expense – motor vehicles	3,105	
	302,625	302,625

Prepare the financial statements of the sole trader for the year ended 30 June 20X8.

Statement of profit or loss for the year ended 30 June 20X8

	£	£
Sales revenue		
Cost of goods sold		
Gross profit		
Total expenses		
Profit/(loss) for the year		

Statement of financial position as at 30 June 20X8

	Cost	Depreciation	Carrying amount
	£	£	£
Non-current assets			
Current assets			
Current liabilities			
Net current assets			
Net assets			
Financed by:			

Task 2.6

A sole trader has prepared his financial statements from his trial balance. Extracts from that trial balance are given below:

	£	£
Sales		184,321
Purchases	91,201	
General expenses	16,422	

You are required to prepare journal entries showing how these accounts would be closed off at the year end.

	Debit	Credit
	£	£

Task 2.7

A trial balance contains the following balances:

	£
Opening inventory	2,000
Closing inventory	4,000
Purchases	20,000
Purchases returns	400
Settlement discounts received	1,600

What is the cost of sales?

£ _____

Task 2.8

For a statement of financial position to balance, which of the following statements is wrong?

✓	
	Net assets = owner's funds
	Net assets = capital + profit + drawings
	Net assets = capital + profit – drawings
	Non-current assets + net current assets = capital + profit – drawings

Chapter 3 – Incomplete records

Task 3.1

On 1 January 20X8, a business had assets of £10,000 and liabilities of £7,000. By 31 December 20X8 it had assets of £15,000 and liabilities of £10,000. The owner had contributed capital of £4,000.

Use the T account below to calculate how much profit or loss the business had made over the year.

£	*1000*

Capital account

	£		£

Task 3.2

The net assets of a business totalled £14,689 at 1 January 20X8 and £19,509 at 31 December 20X8. The owner did not pay any additional capital into the business but did withdraw £9,670 in drawings.

Use the T account below to calculate the profit or loss made by the business in the year.

£	

Capital account

	£		£

Task 3.3

A business has net assets of £31,240 on 31 May 20X8. On 1 June 20X7 the net assets of the business were £26,450. The owner knows that he took £12,300 of drawings out of the business during the year in cash and £560 of goods for his own use.

Use the T account below to calculate the profit or loss made by the business in the year.

£	

Capital account

	£		£

Task 3.4

A business had net assets at the start of the year of £23,695 and at the end of the year of £28,575. The business made a profit of £17,370 for the year.

Use the T account below to calculate the drawings made by the owner in the year.

£	

Capital account

	£		£

Task 3.5

The owner of a small shop provides you with the following information about its transactions for the month of May 20X8:

	£
Till rolls showing amounts paid into till	5,430
Paying in slip stub showing amount paid into bank from till	4,820
Cheques to payables totalling	3,980

The till always has a £100 cash float and the balance on the bank account at 1 May was £368 and at 30 May was £414. The owner has taken cash drawings out of the till and out of the bank account directly.

Use the T accounts below to calculate the drawings made by the owner in the month.

£	

Cash account

£		£

Bank account

£		£

Task 3.6

A small shop keeps a cash float of £250 in the till. The bank statement for the month of March 20X9 shows that the amount of cash paid into the bank for the month was £7,236. The owner keeps a record of the amounts of cash paid directly out of the till and knows that these consisted of wages of £320, cleaning costs of £50 and drawings of £1,050.

Use the T account below to calculate the sales in the month.

£ [   ]

Cash account

	£		£

Task 3.7

A business has a balance on its receivables account of £1,589 at the start of October 20X8 and this has risen to £2,021 by the end of October. The paying in slips for the month show that £5,056 was received from receivables during the month and discounts of £127 were allowed.

Use the T account below to calculate the credit sales in the month.

£ [   ]

Receivables account

	£		£

Task 3.8

The balance on a business's payables account at 1 March 20X9 was £4,266 and by 31 March was £5,111. During the month cheques paid to payables totalled £24,589 and discounts received were £491.

Use the T account below to calculate the credit purchases in the month.

£	

Payables account

	£		£

Task 3.9

A shop operates with a mark-up on cost of 20%. The purchases for the month of May totalled £3,600 and the inventory at the start of May was £640 and at the end of May was £570.

What were the sales for the month?

£	

Task 3.10

A shop operates with a mark-up on cost of 30%. The sales for the period were £5,200 and the inventory at the start and end of the period were £300 and £500.

What were the purchases for the period?

£	

Task 3.11

A shop operates on the basis of a profit margin of 20%. The purchases for the month of April totalled £5,010 and the inventory at the start and the end of the month was £670 and £980 respectively.

What are the sales for the period?

£ [ ]

Task 3.12

Sheena Gordon has been trading for just over 12 months as a dressmaker. She has kept no accounting records at all, and she is worried that she may need professional help to sort out her financial position, and she has approached you.

You meet with Sheena Gordon and discuss the information that you require her to give you. Sometime later, you receive a letter from Sheena Gordon providing you with the information that you requested, as follows:

(i)   She started her business on 1 October 20X7. She opened a business bank account and paid in £5,000 of her savings.

(ii) During October she bought the equipment and the inventory of materials that she needed. The equipment cost £4,000 and the inventory of materials cost £1,800. All of this was paid for out of the business bank account.

(iii) A summary of the business bank account for the twelve months ended 30 September 20X8 showed the following.

	£		£
Capital	5,000	Equipment	4,000
Cash banked	27,000	Opening inventory of materials	1,800
		Purchases of materials	18,450
		General expenses	870
		Drawings	6,200
		Balance c/d	680
	32,000		32,000

(iv) All of the sales are on a cash basis. Some of the cash is paid into the bank account while the rest is used for cash expenses. She has no idea what the total value of her sales is for the year, but she knows that she has spent £3,800 on materials and £490 on general expenses. She took the rest of the cash not banked for her private drawings. She also keeps a cash float of £100.

(v)   The gross profit margin on all sales is 50%.

(vi) She estimates that all the equipment should last for five years. You therefore agree to depreciate it using the straight-line method.

(vii) On 30 September 20X8, the payables for materials amounted to £1,400.

(viii) She estimates that the cost of inventory of materials that she had left at the end of the year was £2,200.

You are required to:

(a) **Calculate the total purchases for the year ended 30 September 20X8**

£ [   ]

(b) **Calculate the total cost of sales for the year ended 30 September 20X8**

£ [   ]

(c) **Calculate the sales for the year ended 30 September 20X8**

£ [   ]

(d) **Show the entries that would appear in Sheena Gordon's cash account**

Cash account

	£		£

(e) **Calculate the total drawings made by Sheena Gordon throughout the year**

£ [   ]

(f) **Calculate the figure for profit for the year ended 30 September 20X8**

£ [   ]

Task 3.13

(a) At 1 January 20X1 suppliers were owed £10,000, by 31 December 20X1 they were owed £8,000. In the year, receivables and payables contras were £3,500, and £350 of debit balances were transferred to receivables. Credit purchases were £60,000 and £2,500 of discounts were received.

What was paid to suppliers during the year?

	✓
£55,650	✓
£56,000	
£56,350	
£58,000	

(b) A business has opening inventory of £30,000 and achieves a mark-up of 25% on cost. Sales totalled £1,000,000, purchases were £840,000.

Calculate closing inventory.

	✓
£30,000	
£40,000	
£120,000	
£70,000	✓

Task 3.14

A sole trader has net assets of £19,000 at 30 April 20X9. During the year to 30 April 20X9 he introduced £9,800 additional capital into the business. Profits were £8,000, of which he withdrew £4,200.

His capital at 1 May 20X8 was:

✓	
	£3,000
✓	£5,400
	£13,000
	£16,600

Chapter 4 – Partnerships

Task 4.1

Jim, Rob and Fiona are in partnership sharing profits in the ratio of 4 : 3 : 2. At 1 January 20X8 the balances on their current accounts were:

Jim	£2,000
Rob	£1,000 (debit)
Fiona	£3,500

During the year to 31 December 20X8 the partnership made a profit of £135,000 and the partners' drawings during the year were:

Jim	£58,000
Rob	£40,000
Fiona	£32,000

Write up the partners' current accounts for the year ended 31 December 20X8. Show the balance b/d on 1 January 20X9.

Current account – Jim

	£		£

Current account – Rob

	£		£

Current account – Fiona

	£		£
	1500		
			———
	———		———

Task 4.2

Josh and Ken are in partnership sharing profits in a ratio of 2 : 1. Ken is allowed a salary of £8,000 per annum and both partners receive interest on their capital balances at 3% per annum. An extract from their trial balance at 30 June 20X8 is given below.

		£
Capital	Josh	40,000
	Ken	25,000
Drawings	Josh	21,000
	Ken	17,400
Current account (credit balances)	Josh	1,300
	Ken	800

The partnership made a profit for the year ended 30 June 20X8 of £39,950.

Write up the profit appropriation account and the partners' current accounts and show the balances that would appear in the statement of financial position for the capital accounts and current accounts.

Profit appropriation account

	£		£

Current account – Josh

	£		£

Current account – Ken

	£		£

Statement of financial position balances

Task 4.3

Jo, Emily and Karen are in partnership sharing profits equally. Emily is allowed a salary of £4,000 per annum and all partners receive interest on their capital balances at 5% per annum.

Given below is the final trial balance of the partnership between Jo, Emily and Karen at 30 June 20X8.

Final trial balance

	Debit £	Credit £
Advertising	3,140	
Bank	1,400	
Capital Jo		25,000
Emily		15,000
Karen		10,000
Payables		33,100
Current accounts Jo		1,000
Emily		540
Karen		230
Receivables	50,000	
Drawings Jo	12,000	
Emily	10,000	
Karen	10,000	
Electricity	4,260	
Furniture and fittings at cost	12,500	
Furniture and fittings – accumulated depreciation		7,025
Insurance	1,800	
Machinery at cost	38,000	
Machinery – accumulated depreciation		23,300
Allowance for doubtful debts		1,500
Cost of goods sold	198,300	
Sales		306,000
Sundry expenses	2,480	
Telephone expenses	2,150	
VAT		1,910
Wages	43,200	
Inventory at 30 June 20X8	24,100	
Depreciation expense – machinery	7,600	
Depreciation expense – furniture and fittings	1,825	
Irrecoverable debts expense	1,550	
Accruals		400
Prepayments	700	
	425,005	425,005

You are required to:

(a) **Prepare the statement of profit or loss for the year ended 30 June 20X8**

(b) **Write up the profit appropriation account and partners' current accounts showing their share of profits and their drawings. Show the balance b/d on 1 July 20X8.**

(c) **Prepare the statement of financial position as at 30 June 20X8**

(a) **Statement of profit or loss for the year ended 30 June 20X8**

	£	£
Sales revenue		
Cost of goods sold		
Gross profit		
Total expenses		
Profit/(loss) for the year		

(b) **Appropriation of profit**

	£	£
Profit for the year		
Profit available for distribution		
Profit share		

Current account – Jo

	£		£

Current account – Emily

	£		£

Current account – Karen

	£		£

(c) **Statement of financial position as at 30 June 20X8**

	Cost	Depreciation	Carrying amount
	£	£	£
Non-current assets			
Current assets			
Current liabilities			
Net current assets			
Net assets			
Financed by:			

Task 4.4

Ian and Max have been in partnership for a number of years sharing profits in the ratio of 2 : 1. The net assets of the partnership total £145,000 and it is believed that in addition the partnership has goodwill of £18,000. Len is to be admitted to the partnership on 1 June 20X8 and is to pay in £32,600 of capital. After Len has been admitted the profits will be shared 2 : 2 : 1.

Write up the partners' capital accounts given below to reflect the goodwill adjustment and the admission of the new partner.

Capital accounts

	Ian £	Max £	Len £		Ian £	Max £	Len £
				Bal b/d	85,000	60,000	

....

Task 4.5

Theo, Deb and Fran have been in partnership for a number of years but on 31 December 20X8 Deb is to retire. The credit balances on the partners' capital and current accounts at that date are:

		£
Capital	Theo	84,000
	Deb	62,000
	Fran	37,000
Current	Theo	4,500
	Deb	1,300
	Fran	6,200

Before the retirement of Deb the partners had shared profits in the ratio of 3 : 2 : 1. However after Deb's retirement the profit sharing ratio between Theo and Fran is to be 2 : 1. The goodwill of the partnership on 31 December 20X8 is estimated to be £54,000. The agreement with Deb is that she will be paid £10,000 at the date of retirement and the remainder of the amount that is due to her will take the form of a loan to the partnership.

Write up the partners' capital and current accounts to reflect Deb's retirement.

Capital accounts

	Theo £	Deb £	Fran £		Theo £	Deb £	Fran £

Current accounts

	Theo £	Deb £	Fran £		Theo £	Deb £	Fran £

Task 4.6

During the year to 30 September 20X8 the partnership of Will and Clare Evans made a profit for the year of £90,000. From 1 October 20X7 until 30 June 20X8 the partnership agreement was as follows:

		Per annum £
Salaries	Will	10,000
	Clare	15,000

Interest on capital 3% of the opening capital balance

Profit share	Will	two-thirds
	Clare	one-third

However on 1 July 20X8 the partnership agreement was changed as follows:

		£
Salaries	Will	12,000
	Clare	20,000

Interest on capital 3% of the opening capital balance

Profit share	Will	three-quarters
	Clare	one-quarter

The opening balances at 1 October 20X7 on their capital and current accounts were as follows:

		£
Capital	Will	80,000
	Clare	50,000
Current	Will	2,000 (credit)
	Clare	3,000 (debit)

During the year ended 30 September 20X8 Will made drawings of £44,000 and Clare made drawings of £37,000.

At 30 June 20X8 the goodwill in the partnership was valued at £60,000. The partners have agreed that goodwill should be reallocated following the change to the partnership agreement.

Prepare the partnership profit appropriation account and the partners' current and capital accounts for the year ended 30 September 20X8.

Profit appropriation account

	1 October 20X7 to 30 June 20X8	1 July 20X8 to 30 Sept 20X8	Total
	£	£	£
	_____	_____	_____
Profit for distribution			
Profit share			
	_____	_____	_____
	_____	_____	_____

Current accounts

	Will £	Clare £		Will £	Clare £
	_____	_____		_____	_____
	_____	_____		_____	_____

Capital accounts

	Will £	Clare £		Will £	Clare £

Task 4.7

Mary Rose, Nelson Victory and Elizabeth Second are in partnership together hiring out river boats. Mary has decided to retire from the partnership at the end of the day on 31 March 20X9. You have been asked to finalise the partnership accounts for the year ended 31 March 20X9 and to make the entries necessary to account for the retirement of Mary from the partnership on that day.

You have been given the following information:

(1) The profit for the year ended 31 March 20X9 was £106,120.

(2) The partners are entitled to the following salaries per annum.

	£
Mary	18,000
Nelson	16,000
Elizabeth	13,000

(3) Interest on capital is to be paid at a rate of 12% on the balance at the beginning of the year on the capital accounts. No interest is paid on the current accounts.

(4) Cash drawings in the year amounted to:

	£
Mary	38,000
Nelson	30,000
Elizabeth	29,000

(5) The balances on the current and capital accounts at 1 April 20X8 were as follows.

Capital accounts		Current accounts	
	£		£
Mary	28,000 (credit)	Mary	£2,500 (credit)
Nelson	26,000 (credit)	Nelson	£2,160 (credit)
Elizabeth	22,000 (credit)	Elizabeth	£1,870 (credit)

(6) The profit-sharing ratios in the partnership are currently:

Mary	4/10
Nelson	3/10
Elizabeth	3/10

On the retirement of Mary, Nelson will put a further £40,000 of capital into the business. The new profit-sharing ratios will be:

Nelson	6/10
Elizabeth	4/10

(7) The goodwill in the partnership is to be valued at £90,000 on 31 March 20X9. No separate account for goodwill is to be maintained in the books of the partnership. Any adjusting entries in respect of goodwill are to be made in the capital accounts of the partners.

(8) Any amounts to the credit of Mary on the date of her retirement should be transferred to a loan account.

You are required to:

(a) Prepare the partners' capital accounts as at 31 March 20X9 showing the adjustments that need to be made on the retirement of Mary from the partnership

(b) Prepare an appropriation account for the partnership for the year ended 31 March 20X9

(c) Prepare the partners' current accounts for the year ended 31 March 20X9

(d) Show the balance on Mary's loan account as at 31 March 20X9

(a) Partners' capital accounts

Partners' capital accounts

	Mary £	Nelson £	Elizabeth £		Mary £	Nelson £	Elizabeth £

(b) **Mary, Nelson and Elizabeth**

Profit appropriation account for the year ended 31 March 20X9

	£	£
Profit for the year		106,120
Profit available for distribution		
Profit share		

(c)

Partners' current accounts

	Mary £	Nelson £	Elizabeth £		Mary £	Nelson £	Elizabeth £
	38ʋʋ	30ʋʋ	29ʋʋ		2,5ʋ	2,16ʋ	18,70
					18ʋʋ	16ʋʋ	13ʋʋ
					3,360	1,920	15,60

(d)

Mary: loan account

	£		£

....

Task 4.8

Fill in the missing word regarding the definition of a partnership.

A partnership is a relationship between persons carrying on a business in common with a view to [   ] .

....

Task 4.9

What is the double entry for drawings made by a partner?

Debit	
Credit	

....

Task 4.10

What is the double entry to record interest earned on partners' capital account balances?

✓		
	Debit	partners' current accounts
	Credit	profit and loss appropriation account
✓	Debit	profit and loss appropriation account
	Credit	partners' current accounts
	Debit	profit and loss appropriation account
	Credit	cash
	Debit	profit and loss appropriation account
	Credit	partners' capital account

....

Task 4.11

You have the following information about a partnership:

The partners are Derek and Eva.

- Fabio was admitted to the partnership on 1 April 20X1 when he introduced £60,000 to the bank account.

- Profit share, effective until 31 March 20X1:

    - Derek   50%
    - Eva   50%

- Profit share, effective from 1 April 20X1:

    - Derek   40%
    - Eva   40%
    - Fabio   20%

- Goodwill was valued at £44,000 on 31 March 20X1.

- Goodwill is to be introduced into the partners' capital accounts on 31 March and then eliminated on 1 April.

(a) **Prepare the capital account for Fabio, the new partner, showing clearly the balance carried down as at 1 April 20X1.**

Capital account – Fabio

	£		£
		Balance b/d	0
	88 w		60 on
	5n 2 o		

(b) **Complete the following sentence by selecting the appropriate phrase from the picklist in each case:**

When a partner retires from a partnership business, the balance on the [▼] must be transferred to the [▼]

Picklist

business bank account
partner's capital account 2
partner's current account 1

Answer bank

Answer bank

Chapter 1

Task 1.1

Balance	Asset ✓	Liability ✓	Income ✓	Expense ✓	Capital ✓
Salaries				✓	
Bank overdraft		✓			
Office costs				✓	
Bank loan		✓			
Capital					✓
Receivables	✓				
Purchases				✓	
Discount received			✓		

Task 1.2

Trial balance	Debit £	Credit £	Asset ✓	Liability ✓	Income ✓	Expense ✓	Capital ✓
Rent cost	11,400					✓	
Sales		143,000			✓		
Opening inventory	2,400					✓	
Payables		6,000		✓			
Purchases	86,200					✓	
Drawings	17,910						✓
Telephone costs	1,250					✓	
Discounts received		80			✓		
Distribution costs	400					✓	
Motor vehicles	32,600		✓				
Receivables	11,900		✓				
Discounts allowed	120					✓	
Capital		40,000					✓
Wages	20,600					✓	
Heat and light	1,600					✓	
Computer	2,400		✓				
Bank	300		✓				
	189,080	189,080					

Task 1.3

Gross profit	£	446,957
Profit for the year	£	254,902

Workings

	£	£
Sales revenue		867,450
Cost of sales:		
Opening inventory	24,578	
Purchases	426,489	
	451,067	
Less: closing inventory	(30,574)	
		(420,493)
Gross profit		446,957
Distribution costs		(104,366)
Administration costs		(87,689)
Profit for the year		254,902

Task 1.4

- Non-current assets
- Current assets – inventories, receivables, bank and cash
- Current liabilities – payables
- Long term liabilities – loans
- Capital
- Profits earned
- Drawings

Task 1.5

Balance	Asset ✓	Liability ✓	Income ✓	Expense ✓	Type of asset/liability
A company car	✓				Non-current asset
Interest on a bank overdraft				✓	
A bank loan repayable in five years		✓			Long-term liability
Petty cash of £25	✓				Current asset
The portion of rent paid covering the period after the statement of financial position date	✓				Prepayment (current asset)
Freehold property	✓				Non-current asset
Payment of wages for a manager with a two year service contract				✓	
An irrecoverable debt written off				✓	

Task 1.6

Statement of financial position (SFP)

A statement of financial position (SFP) is a list of the assets, liabilities and capital of a business at a given moment. Assets are divided into non-current assets and current assets. Liabilities may be current or non-current (long term).

Statement of profit or loss (P/L)

A statement of profit or loss (P/L) matches the revenue earned in a period with the costs incurred in earning it. It is usual to distinguish between a gross profit (sales revenue less the cost of goods sold) and a profit for the year (being the gross profit less the expenses of selling, distribution, administration and so on).

Task 1.7

Materiality

Task 1.8

Relevance

Financial information is said to be relevant if it has the ability to influence the economic decisions of the users of that information and is provided in time to influence those decisions. Where an organisation faces a choice of accounting policies they should choose the one that is more relevant in the context of the final accounts as a whole. Materiality also affects relevance.

Reliability

In the financial statements:

- The figures should represent the substance of the transactions or events

- The figures should be free from bias, or neutral

- The figures should be free from material errors

- A degree of caution should have been applied in making judgements where there is uncertainty

Comparability

Information in financial statements is used by many different people and organisations. It is much more useful to these users if it is comparable over time and also with similar information about other businesses. The selection of appropriate accounting policies and their consistent use should provide such comparability.

Ease of understanding

Accounting policies should be chosen to ensure ease of understanding for users of financial statements. For this purpose users are assumed to have a reasonable knowledge of business and economic activities and accounting and a willingness to study the information diligently.

Task 1.9

Classification	Non-current assets ✓	Current assets ✓	Liabilities ✓
A PC used in the accounts department of a shop	✓		
A PC on sale in an office equipment shop		✓	
Wages due to be paid to staff at the end of the week			✓
A van for sale in a motor dealer's showroom		✓	
A delivery van used in a grocer's business	✓		
An amount owing to a bank for a loan for the acquisition of a van, to be repaid over 9 months			✓

Task 1.10

The trading account shows the ⏍gross⏍ profit for the period.

The bottom line of the statement of profit or loss shows the ⏍profit for the period.⏍

Task 1.11

	Yes ✓	No ✓
Is a bank overdraft a current liability?	✓	

Task 1.12

Which of the following is **not** an accounting concept?

✓	
	Prudence
	Consistency
✓	Depreciation
	Accruals

Chapter 2

Task 2.1

| £ | 62,867 |

Workings

	£
Opening capital	32,569
Profit for the year	67,458
	100,027
Less: drawings (35,480 + 1,680)	37,160
Closing capital	62,867

Task 2.2

Debit	Drawings
Credit	Purchases

Task 2.3

| £ | 79,100 |

Workings

Depreciation charges				
– machinery	=	£140,000 × 20%	=	£28,000
– motor vehicles	=	(£68,000 – 31,200) × 35%	=	£12,880
– furniture and fittings	=	(£23,000 – 13,400) × 20%	=	£1,920

	Cost	Accumulated depreciation	Carrying amount
	£	£	£
Machinery	140,000	92,500	47,500
Motor vehicles	68,000	44,080	23,920
Furniture and fittings	23,000	15,320	7,680
			79,100

Task 2.4

Statement of profit or loss for the year ended 31 May 20X8

	£	£
Sales revenue		369,000
Less: Cost of sales		
Opening inventory	41,000	
Purchases	245,000	
	286,000	
Less: closing inventory	(43,500)	
Cost of goods sold		242,500
Gross profit		126,500
Discounts received		2,000
		128,500
Less: Expenses		
Discounts allowed	2,950	
Electricity	2,950	
Insurance	2,300	
Miscellaneous expenses	1,500	
Motor expenses	3,100	
Rent	3,400	
Telephone costs	1,950	
Wages	52,000	
Depreciation furniture and fittings	2,450	
motor vehicles	7,800	
Irrecoverable debts	1,700	
Total expenses		(82,100)
Profit for the year		46,400

Statement of financial position as at 31 May 20X8

	Cost £	Depreciation £	Carrying amount £
Non-current assets			
Furniture and fittings	24,500	8,550	15,950
Motor vehicles	48,000	29,800	18,200
	72,500	38,350	34,150
Current assets			
Inventory		43,500	
Receivables	60,000		
Less: allowance	1,200		
		58,800	
Prepayments		1,500	
		103,800	
Current liabilities			
Payables	40,800		
Bank overdraft	1,650		
Accruals	1,000		
VAT	4,100		
		47,550	
Net current assets			56,250
Net assets			90,400
Financed by:			
Opening capital			74,000
Profit for the year			46,400
			120,400
Less: drawings			30,000
			90,400

Task 2.5

Statement of profit or loss for the year ended 30 June 20X8

	£	£
Sales revenue		167,400
Cost of goods sold		(118,400)
Gross profit		49,000
Discounts received		2,550
		51,550
Less: Expenses		
Administration expenses	7,490	
Distribution costs	1,530	
Discounts allowed	2,510	
Office costs	1,570	
Selling expenses	6,140	
Wages	16,700	
Irrecoverable debts	2,820	
Depreciation expense:		
machinery	11,680	
motor vehicles	3,105	
Total expenses		(53,545)
Loss for the year		(1,995)

Statement of financial position as at 30 June 20X8

	Cost	Depreciation	Carrying amount
	£	£	£
Non-current assets			
Machinery	58,400	35,040	23,360
Motor vehicles	22,100	12,785	9,315
	80,500	47,825	32,675
Current assets			
Inventory		18,200	
Receivables	14,000		
Less: allowance	(280)		
		13,720	
Prepayments		440	
Bank		2,940	
		35,300	
Current liabilities			
Payables	20,200		
Accruals	680		
VAT	3,690		
		24,570	
Net current assets			10,730
Net assets			43,405
Financed by:			
Capital			60,000
Loss for the year			(1,995)
			58,005
Less: drawings			(14,600)
			43,405

Task 2.6

	Debit	Credit
	£	£
Sales	184,321	
Profit or loss ledger account		184,321
Profit or loss ledger account	91,201	
Purchases		91,201
Profit or loss ledger account	16,422	
General expenses		16,422

Task 2.7

£	17,600

Workings

	£
Purchases	20,000
Less: purchases returns	(400)
	19,600
Add: opening inventory	2,000
Less: closing inventory	(4,000)
Cost of sales	17,600

Task 2.8

✓	
	Net assets = owner's funds
✓	Net assets = capital + profit + drawings
	Net assets = capital + profit – drawings
	Non-current assets + net current assets = capital + profit – drawings

Drawings reduce capital, so they must be deducted.

Chapter 3

Task 3.1

£	2,000 loss

Workings

	£
Assets 1 January 20X8	10,000
Liabilities 1 January 20X8	7,000
Owner's capital at 1 January 20X8	3,000
	£
Assets 31 December 20X8	15,000
Liabilities 31 December 20X8	10,000
Owner's capital at 31 December 20X8	5,000

Capital account

	£		£
Drawings	0	Balance b/d	3,000
Loss (bal fig)	2,000		
Balance c/d	5,000	Capital introduced	4,000
	7,000		7,000

Task 3.2

£	14,490 profit

Workings

Capital account

	£		£
Drawings	9,670	Balance b/d	14,689
Balance c/d	19,509	Profit (bal fig)	14,490
	29,179		29,179

Task 3.3

£	17,650 profit

Workings

Capital account

	£		£
Drawings	12,860	Balance b/d	26,450
Balance c/d	31,240	Profit (bal fig)	17,650
	44,100		44,100

Task 3.4

£	12,490

Workings

Capital account

	£		£
Drawings (bal fig)	12,490	Balance b/d	23,695
Balance c/d	28,575	Profit	17,370
	41,065		41,065

Task 3.5

£	1,404

Workings

Cash account

	£		£
Balance b/d	100	Bankings	4,820
Sales	5,430	Drawings (bal fig)	610
		Balance c/d	100
	5,530		5,530

Bank account

	£		£
Balance b/d	368	Payables	3,980
Bankings	4,820	Drawings (bal fig)	794
		Balance c/d	414
	5,188		5,188

Total drawings	£
Cash	610
Bank	794
	1,404

Task 3.6

£	8,656

Workings

Cash account

	£		£
Balance b/d	250	Bankings	7,236
Sales (bal fig)	8,656	Wages	320
		Cleaning costs	50
		Drawings	1,050
		Balance c/d	250
	8,906		8,906

Task 3.7

£	5,615

Workings

Receivables account

	£		£
Balance b/d	1,589	Bank	5,056
Sales (bal fig)	5,615	Discount allowed	127
		Balance c/d	2,021
	7,204		7,204

Task 3.8

£	25,925

Workings

Payables account

	£		£
Bank	24,589	Balance b/d	4,266
Discounts received	491	Purchases (bal fig)	25,925
Balance c/d	5,111		
	30,191		30,191

Task 3.9

£	4,404

Workings

	£	%
Sales (bal fig)	4,404	120
Cost of sales (640 + 3,600 – 570)	3,670	100
Gross profit	734	20

Task 3.10

£	4,200

Workings

	£	£	%
Sales revenue		5,200	130
Cost of sales			
Opening inventory	300		
Purchases (bal fig)	4,200		
	4,500		
Less: closing inventory	(500)		
Cost of sales (5,200 × 100/130)		4,000	100
Gross profit		1,200	30

Task 3.11

£	5,875

Workings

	£	%
Sales (bal fig)	5,875	100
Cost of sales (670 + 5,010 – 980)	4,700	80
Gross profit	1,175	20

Task 3.12

(a) £ | 25,450

Workings:

	£
Opening inventory	1,800
Payments: bank	18,450
cash	3,800
Payables	1,400
Total purchases	25,450

(b) £ | 23,250

Workings:

	£
Purchases (from (a))	25,450
Closing inventory	(2,200)
Total cost of sales	23,250

(c) £ | 46,500

Workings:

	£
Cost of sales (from (b))	23,250
Total sales (× 2) (gross profit margin 50%)	46,500

(d)

Cash account

	£		£
Sales (from (c))	46,500	Bank account	27,000
		Materials	3,800
		General expenses	490
		Drawings	15,110
		(balancing figure)	
		Bal c/d (float)	100
	46,500		46,500

(e) £ | 21,310

Workings:

	£
Bank account	6,200
Cash account (from (d))	15,110
Total drawings	21,310

(f) | £ | 21,090 |

Workings:

	£	£
Sales (from (c))		46,500
Cost of sales (from (b))		(23,250)
Gross profit		23,250
General expenses (870 + 490)	1,360	
Depreciation (4,000/5)	800	
		(2,160)
Profit for the year		21,090

Task 3.13

(a)

	✓
£55,650	
£56,000	
£56,350	✓
£58,000	

Workings

Payables control account

	£		£
Contra	3,500	Balance b/d	10,000
Discounts received	2,500	Transfers to receivables	350
Cash paid (bal fig)	56,350	Purchases	60,000
Balance c/d	8,000		
	70,350		70,350

(b)

	✓
£30,000	
£40,000	
£120,000	
£70,000	✓

Workings

	£	%
Sales	1,000,000	125
Cost of sales	800,000	100
Opening inventory	30,000	
Purchases	840,000	
	870,000	
Closing inventory (bal fig)	(70,000)	
Cost of sales	800,000	

Task 3.14

✓	
	£3,000
✓	£5,400
	£13,000
	£16,600

Working

	£
Opening capital (balancing figure)	5,400
Capital introduced	9,800
Profits	8,000
	23,200
Drawings	(4,200)
Net assets	19,000

Chapter 4

Task 4.1

Current account – Jim

	£		£
Drawings	58,000	Balance b/d	2,000
Balance c/d	4,000	Profit share (135,000 × 4/9)	60,000
	62,000		62,000
		Balance b/d	4,000

Current account – Rob

	£		£
Balance b/d	1,000	Profit share (135,000 × 3/9)	45,000
Drawings	40,000		
Balance c/d	4,000		
	45,000		45,000
		Balance b/d	4,000

Current account – Fiona

	£		£
Drawings	32,000	Balance b/d	3,500
Balance c/d	1,500	Profit share (135,000 × 2/9)	30,000
	33,500		33,500
		Balance b/d	1,500

Task 4.2

Profit appropriation account

	£		£
Salary – Ken	8,000	Profit for the year b/d	39,950
Interest			
Josh (40,000 × 3%)	1,200		
Ken (25,000 × 3%)	750		
Balance c/d	30,000		
	39,950		39,950
		Profit for distribution	30,000
Profit share			
Josh (30,000 × 2/3)	20,000		
Ken (30,000 × 1/3)	10,000		
	30,000		30,000

Current account – Josh

	£		£
Drawings	21,000	Balance b/d	1,300
Balance c/d	1,500	Profit share (1,200 + 20,000)	21,200
	22,500		22,500
		Balance b/d	1,500

Current account – Ken

	£		£
Drawings	17,400	Balance b/d	800
		Profit share	
Balance c/d	2,150	(8,000 + 750 + 10,000)	18,750
	19,550		19,550
		Balance b/d	2,150

Statement of financial position balances

Capital accounts:

– Josh   £40,000

– Ken   £25,000

Current accounts:

– Josh   £1,500

– Ken   £2,150

Task 4.3

(a) Profit or loss for the year ended 30 June 20X8

	£	£
Sales revenue		306,000
Cost of good sold		(198,300)
Gross profit		107,700
Less: Expenses		
Advertising	3,140	
Electricity	4,260	
Insurance	1,800	
Sundry expenses	2,480	
Telephone expenses	2,150	
Wages	43,200	
Depreciation machinery	7,600	
furniture and fittings	1,825	
Irrecoverable debts	1,550	
Total expenses		(68,005)
Profit for the year		39,695

(b) Appropriation of profit

	£	£
Profit for the year		39,695
Salary – Emily		(4,000)
Interest Jo (25,000 × 5%)		(1,250)
Emily (15,000 × 5%)		(750)
Karen (10,000 × 5%)		(500)
Profit available for distribution		33,195
Profit share (33,195/3)		
Jo		11,065
Emily		11,065
Karen		11,065
		33,195

Current account – Jo

	£		£
Drawings	12,000	Bal b/d	1,000
Bal c/d	1,315	Interest	1,250
		Profit	11,065
	13,315		13,315
		Bal b/d	1,315

Current account – Emily

	£		£
Drawings	10,000	Bal b/d	540
Bal c/d	6,355	Salary	4,000
		Interest	750
		Profit	11,065
	16,355		16,355
		Bal b/d	6,355

Current account – Karen

	£		£
Drawings	10,000	Bal b/d	230
Bal c/d	1,795	Interest	500
		Profit	11,065
	11,795		11,795
		Bal b/d	1,795

(c) **Statement of financial position as at 30 June 20X8**

	Cost	Accumulated depreciation	Carrying amount
	£	£	£
Non-current assets			
Machinery	38,000	23,300	14,700
Furniture and fittings	12,500	7,025	5,475
	50,500	30,325	20,175
Current assets			
Inventory		24,100	
Receivables	50,000		
Less: allowance	1,500		
		48,500	
Prepayments		700	
Bank		1,400	
		74,700	
Current liabilities			
Payables	33,100		
Accruals	400		
VAT	1,910		
		35,410	
Net current assets			39,290
Net assets			59,465
Financed by:			
Capital accounts Jo			25,000
Emily			15,000
Karen			10,000
			50,000
Current accounts Jo	1,315		
Emily	6,355		
Karen	1,795		
			9,465
			59,465

Task 4.4

Capital accounts

	Ian £	Max £	Len £		Ian £	Max £	Len £
				Bal b/d	85,000	60,000	
Goodwill	7,200	7,200	3,600	Goodwill	12,000	6,000	
Balance c/d	89,800	58,800	29,000	Bank			32,600
	97,000	66,000	32,600		97,000	66,000	32,600

Task 4.5

Capital accounts

	Theo £	Deb £	Fran £		Theo £	Deb £	Fran £
				Balance b/d	84,000	62,000	37,000
				Current a/c		1,300	
Goodwill	36,000		18,000	Goodwill	27,000	18,000	9,000
Bank		10,000					
Loan		71,300					
Balance c/d	75,000		28,000				
	111,000	81,300	46,000		111,000	81,300	46,000

Current accounts

	Theo £	Deb £	Fran £		Theo £	Deb £	Fran £
Capital a/c		1,300		Balance b/d	4,500	1,300	6,200
Balance c/d	4,500		6,200				
	4,500	1,300	6,200		4,500	1,300	6,200

Task 4.6

Profit appropriation account

	1 October 20X7 to 30 June 20X8	1 July 20X8 to 30 Sept 20X8	Total
	£	£	£
Profit 9/12 and 3/12 × £90,000	67,500	22,500	90,000
Salaries			
Will (9/12 × 10,000) and (3/12 × 12,000)	(7,500)	(3,000)	(10,500)
Clare (9/12 × 15,000) and (3/12 × 20,000)	(11,250)	(5,000)	(16,250)
Interest			
Will 9/12 and 3/12 × £2,400	(1,800)	(600)	(2,400)
Clare 9/12 and 3/12 × £1,500	(1,125)	(375)	(1,500)
Profit for distribution	45,825	13,525	59,350
Profit share			
Will (2/3 × 45,825) and (3/4 × 13,525)	30,550	10,144	40,694
Clare (1/3 × 45,825) and (1/4 × 13,525)	15,275	3,381	18,656
	45,825	13,525	59,350

Current accounts

	Will	Clare		Will	Clare
	£	£		£	£
Balance b/d		3,000	Balance b/d	2,000	
Drawings	44,000	37,000	Salaries	10,500	16,250
Balance c/d	11,594		Interest	2,400	1,500
			Profit share	40,694	18,656
			Balance c/d		3,594
	55,594	40,000		55,594	40,000

Capital accounts

	Will £	Clare £		Will £	Clare £
			Balance b/d	80,000	50,000
Goodwill	45,000	15,000	Goodwill	40,000	20,000
Balance c/d	75,000	55,000			
	120,000	70,000		120,000	70,000

· ·

Task 4.7

(a) **Partners' capital accounts**

Partners' capital accounts

	Mary £	Nelson £	Elizabeth £		Mary £	Nelson £	Elizabeth £
Goodwill (6:4)	–	54,000	36,000	Balance b/d	28,000	26,000	22,000
Loan				Cash		40,000	
(bal. fig)	69,860	–	–	Goodwill (4:3:3)	36,000	27,000	27,000
Balance c/d	–	39,000	13,000	Current a/c	5,860		
	69,860	93,000	49,000		69,860	93,000	49,000

(b) **Mary, Nelson and Elizabeth**

Profit appropriation account for the year ended 31 March 20X9

	£	£
Profit for the year		106,120
Less: partners' salaries		
Mary	18,000	
Nelson	16,000	
Elizabeth	13,000	
		47,000
Less: interest on capital		
Mary (£28,000 × 12%)	3,360	
Nelson (£26,000 × 12%)	3,120	
Elizabeth (£22,000 × 12%)	2,640	
		9,120
Profit available for distribution		50,000
Profit share		
Mary 4/10		20,000
Nelson 3/10		15,000
Elizabeth 3/10		15,000
		50,000

(c)

Partners' current accounts

	Mary £	Nelson £	Elizabeth £		Mary £	Nelson £	Elizabeth £
Drawings	38,000	30,000	29,000	Balance b/d	2,500	2,160	1,870
Capital a/c	5,860	–	–	Interest on	3,360	3,120	2,640
				capital			
Balance c/d	–	6,280	3,510	Salaries	18,000	16,000	13,000
				Profit	20,000	15,000	15,000
	43,860	36,280	32,510		43,860	36,280	32,510

(d)

Mary: loan account

	£		£
Balance c/d	69,860	Capital a/c	69,860
	69,860		69,860

Task 4.8

profit

Task 4.9

Debit	Current account
Credit	Bank or Purchases

Task 4.10

✓		
	Debit	partners' current accounts
	Credit	profit and loss appropriation account
✓	Debit	profit and loss appropriation account
	Credit	partners' current accounts
	Debit	profit and loss appropriation account
	Credit	cash
	Debit	profit and loss appropriation account
	Credit	partners' capital account

Interest on partners' capital is an appropriation of profit (debit appropriation account). Since partners have earned the money through their investment in the business, their current accounts should be credited with it.

Task 4.11

(a) **Capital account – Fabio**

	£		£
Goodwill	8,800	Balance b/d	0
Balance c/d	51,200	Bank	60,000
	60,000		60,000

(b) When a partner retires from a partnership business, the balance on the partner's current account must be transferred to the partner's capital account.

AAT AQ2013 SAMPLE ASSESSMENT 1 PREPARE FINAL ACCOUNTS FOR SOLE TRADERS AND PARTNERSHIPS

Time allowed: 2 hours

Task 1 (18 marks)

This task is about incomplete records and reconstructing general ledger accounts.

You are working on the accounting records of a sole trader for the year ended 31 March 20X7. You have the following information:

Day-book summaries:	Goods £	VAT £	Total £
Sales	159,000	31,800	190,800
Sales returns	1,600	320	1,920
Purchases	126,000	24,570	150,570
Purchases returns	None		

Further information:	Net £	VAT £	Total £
General expenses	7,360	1,472	8,832

Balances as at:	31 March 20X6 £	31 March 20X7 £
Trade receivables	17,400	18,980
Trade payables	12,250	14,630
Closing inventory	10,380	11,970
VAT	1,704 credit	Not available
Bank	1,327 debit	Not available

- General expenses are not included in the purchases day-book. £8,832 was posted to the general expenses account.

- Cash sales of £4,000 were made, excluding VAT at 20%. The total banked was posted to the cash sales account.

- All purchases are on credit terms.

Receipts and payments recorded in the bank account comprise:	£
Amounts from credit customers	187,300
Amounts to credit suppliers	145,040
Amounts banked from cash sales	4,800
Loan receipt	8,000
Rent paid	6,900
General expenses	8,832
HMRC for VAT – payment	5,886
Drawings	23,000
Wages	15,500

(a) **Find the missing discounts figure by preparing the purchases ledger control account for the year ended 31 March 20X7.**

Purchases ledger control account

	£		£
▼		▼	
▼		▼	
▼		▼	
▼		▼	
	0		0

Drop-down list:

Balance b/d, Balance c/d, Bank, Cash purchases, Cash sales, Discounts allowed, Discounts received, Drawings, General expenses, Inventory, Loan, Purchases day-book, Rent, Sales day-book, Sales returns day-book, Wages, <Empty>

(b) **Find the closing balance on the VAT control account for the year ended 31 March 20X7. Note: The business is not charged VAT on its rent.**

VAT control

	£		£
▼		▼	
▼		▼	
▼		▼	
▼		▼	
▼		▼	
▼		▼	
	0		0

Drop-down list:

Balance b/d, Balance c/d, Bank, Capital, Cash sales, Discounts allowed, Discounts received, Drawings, General expenses, Loan, Purchases day-book, Rent, Sales day-book, Sales returns day-book, Wages, <Empty>

The totals recorded in the cashbook for the year ended 31 March 20X7 were:

Receipts	£200,100
Payments	£205,158

(c) **Assuming there are no year-end adjustments, what will be the opening balance in the cashbook as at 1 April 20X7?**

£ [   ]   [▼]

Drop-down list:

Debit, credit

....

Task 2 (15 marks)

This task is about calculating missing balances and the preparation of financial statements.

You have the following information about a sole trader:

Assets and liabilities as at 1 April 20X6	£
Office equipment at carrying amount	13,800
Inventory	5,850
Bank (debit balance on bank statement)	190
Trade payables	5,370

There were no other assets or liabilities.

(a) **Calculate the following as at 1 April 20X6. Do NOT enter any figures as negative.**

Assets   £ [   ]

Liabilities   £ [   ]

Capital   £ [   ]

During the year ended 31 March 20X7, sales of £63,900 were made. The trader operates with a gross sales margin of 25%.

(b) **Calculate the cost of goods sold for the year ended 31 March 20X7.**

£ [   ]

Purchases for the year were £46,795.

(c) **Calculate the value of closing inventory.**

£ [ ]

The trader now tells you that during the year he has taken some goods for personal use.

(d) **Complete the following statement.**

This means that the inventory figure in the financial statements at 31 March 20X7 will be [▼] the figure calculated in (c) above.

Drop-down list:

Greater than, Less than, The same as

During the year, the trader also introduced a policy of allowing customers to settle their accounts at least one month after the sale was made.

(e) **Which of the following is most likely to be the total on the sales ledger at the end of the financial year? Choose ONE:**

£6,490 [ ]

£63,900 [ ]

£69,900 [ ]

You are now working on the accounts of a different business. This business recently had its offices broken into and lost the computer on which the accounting records are kept, together with the majority of the supporting paperwork and the computer backups.

The business makes all its purchases by cash.

You have been asked to produce some figures for the financial statements. Each source of information below will help find some of the figures that are missing.

(f) **For each source of information, fill in the ONE missing figure that it will help to find. Note: you do not have sufficient information to find all of the missing figures.**

| **Your sources of information:** |

| **The missing figures:** | Physical inventory count | Bank statement | Mark-up percentage |

| Total sales |

| Trade receivables |

| Closing inventory |

| Cash purchases |

| Profit for the year |

Task 3 (18 marks)

This task is about preparing financial statements for sole traders.

You have the following trial balance for a sole trader known as Onyx Trading. All the necessary year-end adjustments have been made.

The following are accounting policies used by Onyx:

- Sales revenue should include sales returns, if any.
- Purchases should include purchases returns and carriage inwards, if any.

(a) **Calculate the sales revenue figure to be included in the statement of profit or loss for Onyx.**

£ [   ]

(b) **Calculate the purchases figure to be included in the statement of profit or loss for Onyx.**

£ [   ]

(c) **Prepare a statement of profit or loss for Onyx Trading for the year ended 31 March 20X7.**

If necessary, use a minus sign to indicate ONLY the following:

- The deduction of an account balance used to make up cost of goods sold
- A loss for the year

Onyx Trading
Trial balance as at 31 March 20X7

	Dr £	Cr £
Accruals		3,000
Allowance for doubtful debts		850
Allowance for doubtful debts adjustment		600
Bank		6,192
Capital		29,000
Carriage inwards	7,530	
Closing inventory	26,100	26,100
Depreciation charges	9,600	
Drawings	20,580	
Furniture at cost	48,000	
Furniture accumulated depreciation		28,800
Office expenses	31,640	
Opening inventory	25,500	
Payroll expenses	16,950	
Prepayments	2,090	
Purchases	146,040	
Purchases ledger control account		21,775
Sales		260,800
Sales ledger control account	30,660	
Sales returns	5,420	
Selling expenses	10,532	
VAT		3,525
TOTAL	**380,642**	**380,642**

Onyx Trading
Statement of profit or loss for the year ended 31 March 20X7

		£	£
Sales revenue			
	▼		
	▼		
	▼		
	▼		
Cost of goods sold			
Gross profit			
Add:			
	▼		
Less:			
	▼		
	▼		
	▼		
	▼		
	▼		
Total expenses			
Profit/loss for the year			

Drop-down list:

Accruals, Allowance for doubtful debts, Allowance for doubtful debts adjustment, Bank, Capital, Closing inventory, Depreciation charges, Drawings, Furniture accumulated depreciation, Furniture at cost, Office expenses, Opening inventory, Payroll expenses, Prepayments, Purchases, Purchases ledger control account, Sales ledger control account, Selling expenses, VAT, <Empty>

(d) **Which of the following regarding the financial statements of a sole trader is TRUE? Choose ONE.**

Drawings are deducted from capital in the statement of financial position. ☐

Drawings are added to profit in the statement of financial position. ☐

Drawings are deducted from sales revenue in the statement of profit or loss. ☐

Drawings are included in expenses in the statement of profit or loss. ☐

Task 4 (24 marks)

This task is about accounting for partnerships. You have the following information:

> Riva, Sam and Terry have been the owners of a partnership business for many years.
>
> On 1 October 20X6, Riva retired from the partnership. Goodwill was valued at £82,000 and has not yet been entered in the accounting records.
>
> Profit share, effective until 30 September 20X6:
>
> - Riva   50%
> - Sam   40%
> - Terry   10%
>
> Profit share, effective from 1 October 20X6:
>
> - Sam   70%
> - Terry   30%
>
> Goodwill is to be introduced into the accounting records on 30 September and then eliminated on 1 October.

(a) **Prepare the goodwill account for the year ended 31 March 20X7 showing clearly the individual entries for the introduction and elimination of goodwill.**

Goodwill account

	£			£
▼			▼	
▼			▼	
▼			▼	
	0			0

Drop-down list:

Balance b/d, Balance c/d, Bank, Capital-Riva, Capital-Sam, Capital-Terry, Current-Riva, Current-Sam, Current-Terry, Drawings, Goodwill, <Empty>

(b) **Which ONE of the following is a key component of partnership financial statements prepared by the accountant?**

Partnership statement of financial position ☐

Partnership Act 1890 ☐

Partnership agreement ☐

Partnership bank statement ☐

You have the following information about another partnership:

- The financial year ends on 31 March.

- The partners at the beginning of the year were Asma and Ben.

- Chris was admitted to the partnership on 1 July 20X6, when the partnership agreement was changed.

- Summary of the partnership agreements:

	Partnership agreement effective until 30 June 20X6		Partnership agreement effective from 1 July 20X6		
	Asma	Ben	Asma	Ben	Chris
Profit share	60%	40%	50%	25%	25%
Salary entitlement per annum	£22,000	£18,000	£22,000	£18,000	£16,000

- Under both agreements, partners are allowed interest on capital. This has been calculated as follows:

Asma   £1,600 for the 12 months ended 31 March 20X7

Ben   £1,200 for the 12 months ended 31 March 20X7

Chris   £800 for the 9 months ended 31 March 20X7

You may assume interest for Asma and Ben accrued evenly across the year.

- Profit for the year ended 31 March 20X7 was £80,000 before appropriations. 80% of the profit was earned in the period after Chris joined the partnership.

(c) You need to prepare the appropriation account for the partnership business for the year ended 31 March 20X7.

- You MUST enter zeros where appropriate in order to obtain full marks.
- Do NOT use brackets, minus signs or dashes.

Partnership appropriation account for the year ended 31 March 20X7

	1 April X6 - 30 June X6 £	1 July X6- 31 March X7 £	Total £
Profit for appropriation			
Salaries:			
Asma			
Ben			
Chris			
Interest on capital:			
Asma			
Ben			
Chris			
Profit available for distribution			

Profit share:			
Asma			
Ben			
Chris			
Total profit distributed			

Task 5 (17 marks)

This task is about preparing a partnership statement of financial position.

You are preparing the statement of financial position for the Onyx partnership as at 31 March 20X7. The partners are Jon and Pat.

You have the final trial balance below. All the necessary year-end adjustments have been made, except for the transfer of £42,600 profit to the current accounts of the partners. Partners share profits and losses in the ratio 2:3, with Pat taking the larger share.

(a) **Calculate the balance of each partner's current account after sharing profits. Indicate whether these balances are DEBIT or CREDIT (the answer fields are not case sensitive).**

		Balance	Debit / Credit
Current account:	Jon £		
Current account:	Pat £		

(b) **Prepare a statement of financial position for the partnership as at 31 March 20X7. You need to use the partners' current account balances that you have just calculated in (a). Do NOT use brackets, minus signs or dashes.**

Onyx Partnership
Trial balance as at 31 March 20X7

	Dr £	Cr £
Accruals		1,740
Administration expenses	33,290	
Advertising expenses	2,000	
Allowance for doubtful debts		2,700
Allowance for doubtful debts adjustment	435	
Bank	13,345	
Capital account-Jon		12,000
Capital account-Pat		18,000
Closing inventory	22,530	22,530
Current account-Jon		360
Current account-Pat	280	

Onyx Partnership
Statement of financial position as at 31 March 20X7

	£	£	£
Non-current assets	Cost	Accumulated depreciation	Carrying amount
▼			
Current assets			
▼			
▼			
▼			
▼			
▼			
Total current assets			

	Dr £	Cr £
Depreciation charges	6,075	
Equipment at cost	32,400	
Equipment accumulated depreciation		14,175
Opening inventory	20,720	
Payroll expenses	10,000	
Payroll liabilities		830
Prepayments	1,200	
Purchases	179,250	
Purchases ledger control account		15,720
Rent	14,800	
Sales		287,340
Sales ledger control account	42,460	
Sales returns	700	
VAT		4,090
TOTAL	**379,485**	**379,485**

	£	£	£
	Cost	Accumulated depreciation	Carrying amount
Current liabilities			
▼			
▼			
▼			
▼			
▼			
Total current liabilities			
Net current assets			
Net assets			
Financed by:	Jon	Pat	Total
▼			
▼			

Drop-down list:

Accruals, Bank, Capital accounts, Current accounts, Equipment, Expenses, Inventory, Payroll expenses, Payroll liabilities, Prepayments, Purchases, Sales, Sales returns, Trade payables, Trade receivables, VAT, <Empty>

AAT AQ2013 SAMPLE ASSESSMENT 1
PREPARE FINAL ACCOUNTS FOR
SOLE TRADERS AND
PARTNERSHIPS

ANSWERS

Task 1 (18 marks)

(a) Purchases ledger control account

		£			£
Bank	▼	145,040	Balance b/d	▼	12,250
Discounts received	▼	3,150	Purchase day-book	▼	150,570
Balance c/d	▼	14,630		▼	
	▼			▼	
		162,820			162,820

(b) VAT control

		£			£
Purchase day-book	▼	24,570	Balance b/d	▼	1,704
General expenses	▼	1,472	Sales day-book	▼	31,800
Bank	▼	5,886	Cash sales	▼	800
Sales returns day-book	▼	320		▼	
Balance c/d	▼	2,056		▼	
	▼			▼	
		34,304			34,304

The totals recorded in the cashbook for the year ended 31 March 20X7 were:

Receipts	£200,100
Payments	£205,158

(c) £ | 3,731 | | credit ▼ |

....

Task 2 (15 marks)

(a) Assets   £ | 19,650 |

     Liabilities £ | 5,560 |

     Capital   £ | 14,090 |

(b) £ | 47,925 |

(c) £ | 4,720 |

(d) This means that the inventory figure in the financial statements at 31 March 20X7 will be | less than ▼ | the figure calculated in (c) above.

(e) £6,490   ✓

    £63,900   ☐

    £69,900   ☐

(f)

Your sources of information:

The missing figures:	Physical inventory count	Bank statement	Mark-up percentage
	Closing inventory	Cash purchases	Total sales

Trade receivables

Profit for the year

Task 3 (18 marks)

(a) £ | 255,380 |

(b) £ | 153,570 |

(c) **Onyx Trading**
Statement of profit or loss for the year ended 31 March 20X7

		£	£
Sales revenue			255,380
Opening inventory	▼	25,500	
Purchases	▼	153,570	
Closing inventory	▼	-26,100	
	▼		
Cost of goods sold			152,970
Gross profit			102,410
Add:			
Allowance for doubtful debts adjustment	▼		600
Less:			
Depreciation charges	▼	9,600	
Office expenses	▼	31,640	
Payroll expenses	▼	16,950	
Selling expenses	▼	10,532	
	▼		
Total expenses			68,722
Profit/(loss) for the year			34,288

(d) Drawings are deducted from capital in the statement of financial position. ☑

Drawings are added to profit in the statement of financial position. ☐

Drawings are deducted from sales revenue in the statement of profit or loss. ☐

Drawings are included in expenses in the statement of profit or loss. ☐

Task 4 (24 marks)

(a) **Goodwill account**

		£			£
Capital – Riva	▼	41,000	Capital – Terry	▼	57,400
Capital – Sam	▼	32,800	Capital – Sam	▼	24,600
Capital – Terry	▼	8,200		▼	
		82,000			82,000

(b) Partnership statement of financial position ✓

Partnership Act 1890 ☐

Partnership agreement ☐

Partnership bank statement ☐

(c) **Partnership appropriation account for the year ended 31 March 20X7**

	1 April X6- 30 June X6 £	1 July X6- 31 March X7 £	Total £
Profit for appropriation	16,000	64,000	80,000
Salaries:			
Asma	5,500	16,500	22,000
Ben	4,500	13,500	18,000
Chris	0	12,000	12,000
Interest on capital:			
Asma	400	1,200	1,600
Ben	300	900	1,200
Chris	0	800	800
Profit available for distribution	5,300	19,100	24,400

Profit share:			
Asma	3,180	9,550	12,730
Ben	2,120	4,775	6,895
Chris	0	4,775	4,775
Total profit distributed	5,300	19,100	24,400

Task 5 (17 marks)

(a)

			Balance	Debit / Credit
Current account:	Jon	£	17,400	Credit
Current account:	Pat	£	25,280	Credit

(b)

Onyx Partnership
Statement of financial position as at 31 March 20X7

		£	£	£
Non-current assets		Cost	Accumulated depreciation	Carrying amount
Equipment	▼	32,400	14,175	18,225
Current assets				
Inventory	▼		22,530	
Trade receivables	▼		39,760	
Prepayments	▼		1,200	
Bank	▼		13,345	
	▼			
Total current assets			76,835	
Current liabilities				
Trade payments	▼	15,720		
VAT	▼	4,090		
Accruals	▼	1,740		
Payroll liabilities	▼	830		
	▼			
Total current liabilities			22,380	
Net current assets				54,455
Net assets				72,680
Financed by:		Jon	Pat	Total
Capital accounts	▼	12,000	18,000	30,000
Current accounts	▼	17,400	25,280	42,680
		29,400	43,280	72,680

AAT AQ2013 SAMPLE ASSESSMENT 2 PREPARE FINAL ACCOUNTS FOR SOLE TRADERS AND PARTNERSHIPS

Time allowed: 2 hours

Task 1 (18 marks)

This task is about incomplete records and reconstructing general ledger accounts.

You are working on the accounting records of a sole trader for the year ended 31 March 20X7. You have the following information:

Day-book summaries	Goods £	VAT £	Total £
Sales	158,000	31,054	189,054
Sales returns	5,030	1,006	6,036
Purchases	91,400	18,280	109,680
Purchases returns	1,270	254	1,524
All sales and purchases are on credit terms.			

Balance as at:	31 March 20X6 £	31 March 20X7 £
Trade receivables	16,835	Not available
Trade payables	11,300	Not available
Closing inventory	8,545	9,780
VAT	1,984 credit	2,621 credit
Bank	1,900 credit	7,052 debit

Receipts and payments recorded in the bank account include:	£
Amounts from credit customers	179,158
Amounts to credit suppliers	107,226
Wages	15,320
General expenses	16,410
HMRC for VAT – payment	8,650
Capital introduced	5,000

Discounts taken by customers for early settlement amounted to £2,730.

(a) Find the closing balance on the sales ledger control account by preparing this account for the year ended 31 March 20X7.

Sales ledger control account

		£			£
	▼			▼	
	▼			▼	
	▼			▼	
	▼			▼	
	▼			▼	
		0			0

Drop-down list:

Balance b/d
Balance c/d
Bank
Capital
Cash purchases
Cash sales
Discounts allowed
Discounts received
Drawings
General expenses
Inventory
Purchases day-book
Purchases returns day-book
Sales day-book
Sales returns day-book
Wages

(b) Find the drawings figure by preparing a summarised bank account for the year ended 31 March 20X7.

Bank

		£			£
	▼			▼	
	▼			▼	
	▼			▼	
	▼			▼	
	▼			▼	
	▼			▼	
	▼			▼	
	▼			▼	
		0			0

Drop-down list:

Balance b/d
Balance c/d
Capital
Cash purchases
Cash sales
Discounts allowed
Discounts received
Drawings
General expenses
Inventory – closing
Inventory – opening
Machinery at cost
Purchases ledger control account
Sales ledger control account
VAT
Wages

Task 2 (15 marks)

This task is about calculating missing balances and the preparation of financial statements.

You have the following information about events on 1 April 20X6.

- A sole trader started business.

- The business was not registered for VAT.

- The sole trader transferred £10,000 of her own money into the business bank account.

- £800 was paid from this account for some office furniture.

- Goods for resale by the business costing £900 were purchased using the trader's personal bank account.

(a) **Complete the capital account as at 1 April 20X6, showing clearly the balance carried down.**

Capital

	£		£
▼		Balance b/d	
▼		▼	
▼		▼	
▼		▼	
	0		0

Drop-down list:

Balance b/d
Balance c/d
Bank
Drawings
Office furniture at cost
Purchases
Purchases ledger control account
Sales
Sales ledger control account
Suspense

At the end of the financial year on 31 March 20X7, you have the following further information:

- Total sales were £66,000
- Total purchases were £59,120.
- A mark-up of 20% on cost was used throughout the year.

(b) Calculate the value of the cost of goods sold for the year ended 31 March 20X7.

£ [   ]

(c) Calculate the value of inventory as at 31 March 20X7.

£ [   ]

The trader's income came only from re-selling goods to customers and there were business expenses during the year. Your assistant has prepared draft financial statements, but unfortunately, the last line of his report has not printed properly.

(d) Taking into account the information you have, which of the following is most likely to be true?

Profit for the year was £1,100	☐
Profit for the year was £11,000	☐

The trader took drawings from the business during the year.

Now complete the following:

This [▼] explain the profit figure above.

Drop-down list:

can
cannot

You are now working for another client.

You have an initial trial balance. The totals are as follows:

Debit side   £162,638   Credit side   £163,628

(e) Which ONE of the following errors could explain this?

An invoice to a customer has been omitted from the subsidiary ledger account.	☐
A prepayment has been duplicated in the correct expense account and omitted from the other side.	☐
The discounts received figure has been posted only to the purchases ledger control account.	☐
The journals for an accrual has been posted the wrong way round.	☐

Task 3 (18 marks)

This task is about preparing financial statements for sole traders.

You have the following trial balance for a sole trader known as Onyx Trading.

All the necessary year end adjustments have been made.

The following are accounting policies used by Onyx:

- Sales revenue should include sales returns, if any.
- Purchases should include purchases returns and carriage inwards, if any.

(a) Calculate the sales revenue figure to be included in the statement of profit or loss for Onyx.

£ [   ]

(b) Calculate the purchases figure to be included in the statement of profit or loss for Onyx.

£ [   ]

(c) Prepare as statement of profit or loss for Onyx Trading for the year ended 31 March 20X7.

If necessary, use a minus sign to indicate ONLY the following:

- The deduction of an account balance used to make up cost of goods sold
- A loss for the year

Onyx Trading
Trial balance as at 31 March 20X7

	Dr £	Cr £
Accruals		1,800
Bank		2,206
Capital		25,000
Carriage inwards	3,230	
Cash	200	
Closing inventory	13,740	13,740
Depreciation charges	5,200	
Drawings	12,000	
Equipment at cost	26,000	
Equipment accumulated depreciation		20,800
General expenses	31,420	
Interest paid	1,050	
Irrecoverable debts	4,000	
Loan		7,000
Opening inventory	18,590	
Prepayments	400	
Purchases	102,440	
Purchases ledger control account		18,740
Sales		187,230
Sales ledger control account	23,500	
Sales returns	11,800	
VAT		1,054
Wages	24,000	
Total	277,570	277,570

Onyx Trading
Statement of profit or loss for the year ended 31 March 20X7

	£	£
Sales revenue		
▼		
▼		
▼		
▼		
Cost of goods sold		
Gross profit		
Less:		
▼		
▼		
▼		
▼		
▼		
▼		
Total expenses		
Profit/(loss) for the year		

Drop-down list:

Accruals
Bank
Cash
Closing inventory
Depreciation charges
Drawings
Equipment accumulated depreciation
Equipment at cost
General expenses
Interest paid
Irrecoverable debts
Loan
Opening inventory
Prepayments
Purchases
Purchases ledger control account
Sales ledger control account
VAT
Wages

You are given the following information about another sole trader:

- The business started trading on 1 January 20X7 when the owner paid £25,000 into the business bank account.

- Gross profit for the year ended 31 December 20X7 was £49,000.

- Profit for the year ended 31 December 20X7 was £19,000.

- Drawings during the year ended 31 December 20X7 were £16,000.

(d) Calculate the balance on the capital account as at 31 December 20X7.

Capital as at 31 December 20X7: £ [   ]

Task 4 (24 marks)

This task is about accounting for partnerships.

You have the following information about a partnership:

> Riva and Sam have been the owners of a partnership business for many years, sharing profits and losses in the ratio 3:2, with Riva receiving the larger share.
>
> On 1 January 20X7, the partnership agreement was changed so that Riva and Sam will share profits and losses in the ratio 2:1, with Riva receiving the larger share.
>
> Goodwill was valued at £72,000 at this date. No entries for goodwill have yet been made in the partnership accounting records.

(a) Show the entries required to introduce the goodwill into the partnership accounting records on 1 January 20X7.

Account name		Amount £	Debit	Credit
	▼			
	▼			
	▼			

Drop-down list:

Balance b/d
Balance c/d
Bank
Capital – Riva
Capital – Sam
Current – Riva
Current – Sam
Drawings
Goodwill

(b) Which of the following should be included in a partnership agreement? Choose ONE:

The partnership appropriation account.	☐
Capital and current accounts for each partner.	☐
Salaries and wages to be paid to all employees.	☐
The rate at which interest is to be allowed on capital.	☐

You have the following information about a partnerships business:

- The financial year ends on 31 March.

- The partners throughout the year were Asma, Ben and Chris.

- The partnerships agreement was changed on 1 October 20X6.

- Ben and Chris each introduced a further £10,000 capital into the bank account on 1 October 20X6.

- Goodwill was valued at £80,000 on 1 October 20X6.

- There was no interest on drawings.

	Asma	Ben	Chris
Profit share, effective until 30 September 20X6	40%	30%	30%
Profit share, effective from 1 October 20X6	30%	35%	35%
Capital account balances at 1 April 20X6	£40,000	£30,000	£30,000
Current account balances at 1 April 20X6	£1,160 credit	£420 credit	£2,570 credit
Drawings for the year ended 31 March 20X7	£3,500 each month	£38,000	£40,000

The appropriation account for the year ended 31 March 20X7 has already been prepared by the accountant.

Partnership appropriation account for the year ended 31 March 20X7

	1 April X6 – 30 September X6 £	1 October X6 – 30 March X6 £	Total £
Profit for appropriation	65,000	65,000	130,000
Salaries:			
Asma	14,000	0	14,000
Ben	10,500	10,500	21,000
Chris	11,000	11,000	22,000
Interest on capital:			
Asma	1,300	1,560	2,860
Ben	900	1,080	1,980
Chris	900	1,080	1,980
Profit available for distribution	26,400	39,780	66,180
Profit shares:			
Asma	10,560	11,934	22,494
Ben	7,920	13,923	21,843
Chris	7,920	13,923	21,843
Total profit distributed	26,400	39,780	66,180

(c) Prepare the current accounts for the partners for the year ended 31 March 20X7. Show clearly the balance carried down. You MUST enter zeros where appropriate in order to obtain full marks. Do NOT use brackets, minus signs or dashes.

Current accounts

	Asma £	Ben £	Chris £		Asma £	Ben £	Chris £
▼				▼			
▼				▼			
▼				▼			
▼				▼			
▼				▼			
▼				▼			
	0	0	0		0	0	0

Drop-down list:

Balance b/d
Balance c/d
Capital – Asma
Capital – Ben
Capital – Chris
Current – Asma
Current – Ben
Current – Chris
Drawings
Goodwill
Interest on capital
Salaries
Share of profit or loss

Task 5 (17 marks)

This task is about preparing a partnership statement of financial position.

You are preparing the statement of financial position for the Onyx partnership for the year end 31 March 20X7.

The partners are Jon and Pat.

You have the final trial balance below. All the necessary year end adjustments have been made, except for the transfer of £40,400 profit to the current accounts of the partners. Partners share profits and losses in the ratio 60:40, with Jon taking the larger share.

(a) **Calculate the balance of each partner's current account after sharing profits. Indicate whether these balance are DEBIT or CREDIT by writing either word in the appropriate field (the answer fields are not case sensitive).**

		Balance	Debit / Credit
Current account:	Jon £		
Current account:	Pat £		

(b) **Prepare a statement of financial position for the partnership as at 31 March 20X7. You need to use the partners' current account balances that you have just calculated in (a). Do NOT use brackets, minus signs or dashes.**

Onyx Trading
Trial balance as at 31 March 20X7

	Dr £	Cr £
Accruals		1,400
Allowance for doubtful debts		950
Allowance for doubtful debts adjustment		120
Bank	13,460	
Capital account – Jon		22,000
Capital account – Pat		14,000
Carriage inwards	6,852	
Cash	320	
Closing inventory	24,380	24,380
Current account – Jon	1,562	
Current account – Pat	1,412	
Depreciation charges	7,080	
Hire purchase (final payment 31/05/X7)		3,200
Interest paid	294	
Office equipment at cost	35,400	
Office equipment accumulated depreciation		14,160
Office expenses	41,576	
Opening inventory	25,870	
Purchases	146,388	
Purchases ledger control account		17,635
Sales		269,127
Sales ledger control account	40,083	
Travel expenses	10,567	
VAT		2,872
Wages	14,600	
Total	369,844	369,844

Onyx Trading
Statement of financial position as at 31 March 20X7

	£	£	£
Non-current assets	Cost	Accumulated Depreciation	Carrying amount
▼			
Current assets			
▼			
▼			
▼			
▼			
▼			
Total current assets			
Current liabilities			
▼			
▼			
▼			
▼			
▼			
Total current liabilities			
Net current assets			
Net assets			
Financed by:	Jon	Pat	Total
▼			
▼			

Drop-down list:

Accruals
Bank
Capital accounts
Carriage inwards
Cash
Current accounts

Expenses
Hire purchase
Inventory
Office equipment
Purchases
Sales
Trade payables
Trade receivables
VAT
Wages

AAT AQ2013 SAMPLE ASSESSMENT 2 PREPARE FINAL ACCOUNTS FOR SOLE TRADERS AND PARTNERSHIPS

ANSWERS

Task 1 (18 marks)

(a) Sales ledger control account

	£		£
Balance b/d	16,835	Bank	179,158
Sales day-book	189,054	Sales returns day-book	6,036
		Discounts allowed	2,730
		Balance c/d	17,965
	205,889		205,889

(b) Bank

	£		£
Sales ledger control account	179,158	Balance b/d	1,900
Capital	5,000	Wages	15,320
		General expenses	16,410
		Purchases ledger control account	107,226
		VAT	8,650
		Drawings	27,600
		Balance c/d	7,052
	184,158		184,158

Task 2 (15 marks)

(a) **Capital**

	£		£
Balance c/d	10,900	Balance b/d	0
		Bank	10,000
		Purchases	900
	10,900		10,900

(b) £ | 55,000

£66,000/1.2 = £55,000

(c) £ | 4,120

£59,120 – £55,000 = £4,120

(d) Profit for the year was £1,100   ✓

Profit for the year was £11,000   ☐

The trader took drawings from the business during the year.

Now complete the following:

This | cannot | explain the profit figure above.

Note: Gross profit is £11,000 (£66,000 – 55,000). There are business expenses, therefore the profit for the year must be less than £11,000.

Drawings are not included as expenses in profit or loss.

(e) An invoice to a customer has been omitted from the subsidiary ledger account.   ☐

A prepayment has been duplicated in the correct expense account and omitted from the other side.   ✓

The discounts received figure has been posted only to the purchases ledger control account.   ☐

The journal for an accrual has been posted the wrong way round.   ☐

Task 3 (18 marks)

(a) £ | 175,430 |

£187,230 – £11,800

(b) £ | 105,670 |

£102,440 + £3,230

(c) **Onyx Trading**

Statement of profit or loss for the year ended 31 March 20X7

	£	£
Sales revenue		175,430
Opening inventory	18,590	
Purchases	105,670	
Closing inventory	–13,740	
Cost of goods sold		110,520
Gross profit		64,910
Less:		
Depreciation charges	5,200	
General expenses	31,420	
Interest paid	1,050	
Wages	24,000	
Irrecoverable debts	4,000	
Total expenses		65,670
Profit/(loss) for the year		–760

(d) Capital as at 31 December 20X7: £ | 28,000 |

£25,000 + £19,000 – £16,000 = £28,000

Task 4 (24 marks)

(a)

Account name	Amount £	Debit	Credit
Goodwill	72,000	✓	
Capital – Riva*	43,200		✓
Capital – Sam**	28,800		✓

*Riva £72,000/5 × 3 = £43,200

**Sam £72,000/5 × 2 = £28,800

(b)

The partnership appropriation account.	☐
Capital and current accounts for each partner.	☐
Salaries and wages to be paid to all employees.	☐
The rate at which interest is to be allowed on capital.	✓

(c) **Current accounts**

	Asma £	Ben £	Chris £		Asma £	Ben £	Chris £
Drawings (W)	42,000	38,000	40,000	Balance b/d	1,160	420	2,570
Balance c/d	0	7,243	8,393	Salaries	14,000	21,000	22,000
				Interest on capital	2,860	1,980	1,980
				Share of profit or loss	22,494	21,843	21,843
				Balance c/d	1,486	0	0
	42,000	45,243	48,393		42,000	45,243	48,393

Workings:

Asma: £3,500 × 12 months = £42,000

Drawings for Ben and Chris taken from question

Task 5 (17 marks)

(a)

			Balance	Debit / Credit
Current account:	Jon	£	22,678	credit
Current account:	Pat	£	14,748	credit

Workings:

Jon: (£40,400 × 60%) − £1,562 = £22,678

Pat: (£40,400 × 40%) − £1,412 = £14,748

(b) **Onyx Trading**
Statement of financial position as at 31 March 20X7

	£	£	£
Non-current assets	Cost	Accumulated Depreciation	Carrying amount
Office equipment	35,400	14,160	21,240
Current assets			
Inventory		24,380	
Trade receivables*		39,133	
Cash		320	
Bank		13,460	
Total current assets		77,293	
Current liabilities			
Trade payables	17,635		
VAT	2,872		
Accruals	1,400		
Hire purchase	3,200		
Total current liabilities		25,107	
Net current assets			52,186
Net assets			73,426
Financed by:	**Jon**	**Pat**	**Total**
Capital accounts	22,000	14,000	36,000
Current accounts	22,678	14,748	37,426
	44,678	28,748	73,426

* £40,083 – £950 = £39,133

BPP PRACTICE ASSESSMENT 1
PREPARE FINAL ACCOUNTS FOR SOLE TRADERS AND PARTNERSHIPS

Time allowed: 2 hours

Task 1

This task is about incomplete records and reconstructing general ledger accounts.

You are working on the financial statements of a business for the year ended 31 March 20X1. You have the following information:

Day book summaries	Goods	VAT	Total
	£	£	£
Sales	125,400	25,080	150,480
Purchases	76,000	15,200	91,200

Balances as at	31 March X0	31 March X1
	£	£
Trade receivables	16,360	15,270
Trade payables	13,280	12,950
Cash in till	300	250

You also find receipts in the cash till for cash purchases of £400.

Bank summary	Dr £		Cr £
Cash banked from till	2,900	Balance b/d	850
Trade receivables	142,650	Administration expenses	3,280
Interest received	520	Trade payables	92,330
		HMRC for VAT	6,820
		Drawings	2,900
		Payroll expenses	12,550
		Balance c/d	27,340
	146,070		146,070

(a) **Using the figures given above, prepare the sales ledger control account for the year ended 31 March 20X1. Show clearly discounts allowed as the balancing figure.**

Sales ledger control account

	£		£

Picklist:

Balance b/d
Balance c/d
Bank
Capital
Cash purchases
Cash sales
Discounts allowed
Discounts received
Drawings
General expenses
Inventory
Purchases day-book
Purchases returns day-book
Sales day-book
Sales returns day-book
Wages

(b) **Find the figure for cash sales by preparing the cash in till account for the year ended 31 March 20X1. Use the figures given on the previous page.**

Note: The business does not charge VAT on its cash sales.

Cash in till

	£		£

You are given the following information about a different sole trader as at 1 November 20XX:

The value of assets and liabilities were:

- Non-current assets at net book value   £17,250
- Trade receivables   £6,250
- Cash at bank   £1,280
- Capital   £21,000

There were no other assets or liabilities.

(c) **Calculate the trade payables account balance as at 1 November 20XX.**

£ [   ]

(d) **On 30 April 20X0, cash is paid to a credit supplier, with some discount taken. Tick the boxes to show what effect this transaction will have on the balances. You must choose ONE answer for EACH line.**

Balances	Debit ✓	Credit ✓	No change ✓
Income			
Trade receivables			
Trade payables			
Bank			
Expenses			

(e) **Which TWO of the following are accurate representations of the accounting equation? Choose TWO answers.**

	✓
Assets + Liabilities = Capital	
Assets – Liabilities = Capital	✓
Assets = Liabilities – Capital	
Assets = Liabilities + Capital	✓

Task 2

This task is about calculating missing balances and the preparation of financial statements.

You have the following information about a sole trader on 1 January 20X4.

- The sole trader started a business and transferred £8,000 of her own money into the business bank account.

- £2,000 was paid from the sole trader's personal credit card for a computer.

- Goods for resale by the business costing £1,500 were purchased from the business bank account.

(a) **Complete the capital account as at 1 January 20X4, showing clearly the balance carried down.**

Capital

	£			£
▼		Balance b/d		
▼			▼	9 ow
▼			▼	
▼			▼	
	0			0

Picklist:

Balance b/d
Balance c/d
Bank
Drawings
Computers at cost
Purchases
Purchases ledger control account
Sales
Sales ledger control account
Suspense

At the end of the financial year on 31 December 20X4, you have the following further information:

- Total sales were £45,000.
- Total purchases were £40,000.
- A mark-up of 25% on cost was used throughout the year.

(b) **Calculate the value of the cost of goods sold for the year ended 31 December 20X4.**

£ 36000

125   45 ow
100
25

(c) **Calculate the value of inventory as at 31 December 20X4.**

£ 4000

The trader rented a premises on a busy high street. Her income came only from selling goods in this store.

(d) **Taking into account the information you have, which of the following is most likely to be true?**

Loss for the year was £9,000	☐
Profit for the year was £9,000	☐

The trader took drawings from the business during the year.

Now complete the following:

This [▼] explain the profit figure above.

Picklist:

can
cannot ✓

(e) **Indicate where the inventory balance should be shown in the financial statements. Choose ONE from:**

	✓
Non-current assets	
Current assets	
Current liabilities	
Non-current liabilities	

Task 3

This task is about preparing financial statements for sole traders.

You have the following trial balance for a sole trader, Martha Tidfill. All the necessary year-end adjustments have been made.

(a) **Prepare a statement of profit or loss for the business for the year ended 31 August 20X4.**

Martha Tidfill
Trial balance as at 31 August 20X4

	Dr £	Cr £
Accruals		1,250
Bank	2,190	
Capital		20,000
Closing inventory	15,200	15,200
Depreciation expense	4,750	
Discounts allowed	1,920	
Drawings	15,000	
Heat and light	11,620	
Motor vehicles accumulated depreciation		7,600
Motor vehicles at cost	25,400	
Office costs	27,690	
Opening inventory	17,690	
Prepayments	1,120	
Purchases	105,280	
Purchases ledger control account		18,280
Sales		199,560
Sales ledger control account	17,960	
VAT		3,920
Wages	19,990	
	265,810	265,810

Martha Tidfill
Statement of profit or loss for the year ended 31 August 20X4

	£	£
Sales revenue		
Cost of goods sold		
Gross profit		
Total expenses		
Profit/(loss) for the year		

(b) **Indicate where the accruals balance should be shown in the financial statements. Choose ONE from:**

	✓
Non-current assets	
Current assets	
Current liabilities	✓
Non-current liabilities	

Task 4

This task is about partnership accounts.

You have the following information about a partnership business:

- The financial year ends on 31 July.

- The partners at the beginning of the year were Grace and Harry.

- Jamal was admitted to the partnership on 1 February 20X6.

- Partners' annual salaries, effective to 31 January 20X6:

  - Grace   £15,600
  - Harry   £19,200
  - Jamal   Nil

- Partners' annual salaries, effective from 1 February 20X6:

  - Grace   £13,200
  - Harry   £16,800
  - Jamal   £6,000

- Partners' interest on capital:

  - Grace   £800 per full year
  - Harry   £1,000 per full year
  - Jamal   £500 per full year

- Profit share, effective until 31 January 20X6:

  - Grace   30%
  - Harry   70%

- Profit share, effective from 1 February 20X6:

  - Grace   40%
  - Harry   50%
  - Jamal   10%

Profit for the year ended 31 July 20X6 was £120,000. You can assume that profits accrued evenly during the year.

Prepare the appropriation account for the partnership for the year ended 31 July 20X6.

Partnership appropriation account for the year ended 31 July 20X6

	1 August X5 – 31 January X6 £	1 February X6 – 31 July X6 £	Total £
Profit for the year			
Salaries:			
Grace			
Harry			
Jamal			
Interest on capital:			
Grace			
Harry			
Jamal			
Profit available for distribution			

Profit share			
Grace			
Harry			
Jamal			
Total profit distributed			

Task 5

Partnership statement of financial position

This task is about preparing a partnership statement of financial position.

You are preparing the statement of financial position for the Jessop Partnership for the year ended 31 October 20X7. The partners are Malcolm and Rose.

All the necessary year end adjustments have been made, except for the transfer of profit to the current accounts of the partners.

Before sharing profits the balances of the partners' current accounts are:

- Malcolm £400 debit
- Rose £230 credit

Each partner is entitled to £7,250 profit share.

(a) **Calculate the credit balance of each partner's current account after sharing profits. Fill in the answers below.**

Current account balance: Malcolm	£	
Current account balance: Rose	£	

Note: these balances will need to be transferred into the statement of financial position of the partnership which follows.

You have the following trial balance. All the necessary year-end adjustments have been made.

(b) **Prepare a statement of financial position for the partnership as at 31 October 20X7. You need to use the partners' current account balances that you have just calculated. Do NOT use brackets, minus signs or dashes.**

Jessop Partnership
Trial balance as at 31 October 20X7

	Dr £	Cr £
Accruals		970
Allowance for doubtful debts		1,280
Allowance for doubtful debts adjustment	130	
Bank		2,140
Capital – Malcolm		18,000
Capital – Rose		22,000
Cash	250	
Closing inventory	9,450	9,450
Current account – Malcolm	400	
Current account – Rose		230
Depreciation expense	2,440	
Disposal of non-current asset	2,100	
Furniture & fittings accumulated depreciation		9,240
Furniture & fittings at cost	32,980	
Marketing	17,930	
Opening inventory	21,780	
Purchases	88,810	
Purchases ledger control account		7,620
Sales		179,610
Sales ledger control account	35,090	
Wages	41,370	
VAT		2,190
Total	252,730	252,730

Jessop Partnership
Statement of financial position as at 31 October 20X7

	Cost £	Depreciation £	Carrying amount £
Non-current assets			
Current assets			
Current liabilities			
Net current assets			
Net assets			
Financed by:	Malcolm	Rose	Total

BPP PRACTICE ASSESSMENT 1 PREPARE FINAL ACCOUNTS FOR SOLE TRADERS AND PARTNERSHIPS

ANSWERS

Task 1

(a) Sales ledger control account

	£		£
Balance b/d	16,360	Bank	142,650
Sales day book	150,480	Discounts allowed	8,920
		Balance c/d	15,270
	166,840		166,840

(b) Cash in till

	£		£
Balance b/d	300	Cash purchases	400
Cash sales	3,250	Cash banked	2,900
		Balance c/d	250
	3,550		3,550

(c)

£	3,780

(17,250 + 6,250 + 1,280 – 21,000)

(d)

Balances	Debit ✓	Credit ✓	No change ✓
Income		✓	
Trade receivables			✓
Trade payables	✓		
Bank		✓	
Expenses			✓

(e)

	✓
Assets + Liabilities = Capital	
Assets – Liabilities = Capital	✓
Assets = Liabilities - Capital	
Assets = Liabilities + Capital	✓

Task 2

(a) **Capital**

	£		£
		Balance b/d	0
		Bank	8,000
Balance c/d	10,000	Computers	2,000
	10,000		10,000

(b) £ | 36,000 |

(c) £ | 4,000 |

(d) Loss for the year was £9,000   ✓

Profit for the year was £9,000   ☐

This | cannot | explain the profit figure above.

Note: Gross profit is £9,000 (£45,000 – £36,000). The business premises is rented, therefore rent is an expense, which means that the profit for the year is not £9,000.

Drawings are not included as expenses in profit or loss.

(e)

	✓
Non-current assets	
Current assets	✓
Current liabilities	
Non-current liabilities	

Task 3

(a)

Martha Tidfill
Statement of profit or loss for the year ended 31 August 20X4

	£	£
Sales revenue		199,560
Opening inventory	17,690	
Purchases	105,280	
Closing inventory	(15,200)	
Cost of goods sold		(107,770)
Gross profit		91,790
Less:		
Depreciation expense	4,750	
Discounts allowed	1,920	
Heat and light	11,620	
Office costs	27,690	
Wages	19,990	
Total expenses		(65,970)
Profit for the year		25,820

(b)

	✓
Non-current assets	
Current assets	
Current liabilities	✓
Non-current liabilities	

Task 4

Partnership appropriation account for the year ended 31 July 20X6

	1 August X5 – 31 January X6 £	1 February X6 – 31 July X6 £	Total £
Profit for the year	60,000	60,000	120,000
Salaries:			
Grace	7,800	6,600	14,400
Harry	9,600	8,400	18,000
Jamal	0	3,000	3,000
Interest on capital:			
Grace	400	400	800
Harry	500	500	1,000
Jamal	0	250	250
Profit available for distribution	41,700	40,850	82,550

Profit share			
Grace	12,510	16,340	28,850
Harry	29,190	20,425	49,615
Jamal		4,085	4,085
Total profit distributed	41,700	40,850	82,550

Task 5

(a)

Current account balance: Malcolm	£	6,850
Current account balance: Rose	£	7,480

(b) **Jessop Partnership**
Statement of financial position as at 31 October 20X7

	Cost £	Depreciation £	Carrying amount £
Non-current assets	32,980	9,240	23,740
Current assets			
Inventory		9,450	
Receivables		33,810	
Cash		250	
		43,510	
Current liabilities			
Accruals	970		
Payables	7,620		
Bank overdraft	2,140		
VAT	2,190		
		12,920	
Net current assets			30,590
Net assets			54,330
Financed by:	**Malcolm**	**Rose**	**Total**
Capital accounts	18,000	22,000	40,000
Current accounts	6,850	7,480	14,330
			54,330

BPP PRACTICE ASSESSMENT 2
PREPARE FINAL ACCOUNTS FOR SOLE TRADERS AND PARTNERSHIPS

Time allowed: 2 hours

Task 1

This task is about incomplete records and reconstructing general ledger accounts.

You are working on the accounting records of a sole trader for the year ended 31 May 20X4. You have the following information:

Day-book summaries:	Goods £	VAT £	Total £
Sales	89,000	17,800	106,800
Sales returns	2,500	500	3,000
Purchases	56,000	11,200	67,200
Purchases returns	None		

Further information:	Net £	VAT £	Total £
General expenses	1,050	210	1,260

Balances as at:	31 May 20X3 £	31 May 20X4 £
Trade receivables	13,000	8,500
Trade payables	9,250	11,250
Closing inventory	3,260	4,650
VAT	555 credit	Not available
Bank	Not available	10,500 debit

- Cash sales of £1,000 were made, excluding VAT at 20%. The total banked was posted to the cash sales account.

- All purchases are on credit terms.

Receipts and payments recorded in the bank account comprise:	£
Amounts from credit customers	98,000
Amounts to credit suppliers	60,300
Amounts banked from cash sales	4,800
Loan receipt	3,000
Rent paid	6,350
General expenses	1,260
HMRC for VAT – payment	1,500
Drawings	12,000
Wages	13,000

(a) **Find the missing discounts figure by preparing the purchases ledger control account for the year ended 31 May 20X4.**

Purchases ledger control account

	£		£
▽		▽	
▽		▽	
▽		▽	
▽		▽	
	0		0

Picklist:

Balance b/d, Balance c/d, Bank, Cash purchases, Cash sales, Discounts allowed, Discounts received, Drawings, General expenses, Inventory, Loan, Purchases day-book, Rent, Sales day-book, Sales returns day-book, Wages, <Empty>

(b) **Find the closing balance on the VAT control account for the year ended 31 May 20X4. Note: The business is not charged VAT on its rent.**

VAT control

	£		£
▽		▽	
▽		▽	
▽		▽	
▽		▽	
▽		▽	
▽		▽	

Picklist:

Balance b/d, Balance c/d, Bank, Capital, Cash sales, Discounts allowed, Discounts received, Drawings, General expenses, Loan, Purchases day-book, Rent, Sales day-book, Sales returns day-book, Wages, <Empty>

The totals recorded in the cashbook for the year ended 31 May 20X4 were:

Receipts	£105,800
Payments	£94,410

(c) **Assuming there are no year-end adjustments, what was the opening balance in the cashbook as at 31 May 20X3?**

£ [   ] [▼]

Picklist:

Debit, credit

Task 2

This task is about calculating missing balances and the preparation of financial statements.

(a) On 1 January 20X8, a business had assets of £20,000 and liabilities of £14,000. By 31 December 20X8 it had assets of £30,000 and liabilities of £20,000. The owner had contributed capital of £8,000 during the year.

Use the T account below to calculate how much profit or loss the business had made over the year.

£ [4 000 . Loss]

Capital account

	£		£
	___		___
	═══		═══

You are given the following information about a different business, a shop, for one financial year:

Sales were £95,200 in the year, all at a mark-up of 60%. The opening inventory was £22,560 and the closing inventory was £18,420.

160 95200
100
60

(b) **Calculate the cost of goods sold figure for the year.**

£ [59500]

(c) **Calculate the purchases figure for the year.**

£ [55360]

(d) **Identify whether each of the following balances is presented as a current asset, a current liability or neither on the face of the statement of financial position.**

Balances	Current asset ✓	Current liability ✓	Neither ✓
Accrual		✓	
Opening inventory			✓
Prepayment	✓		
Loan from bank payable in five years			✓
Bank overdraft		✓	

(e) **Which of the following is best described as a current liability? Choose ONE answer.**

	✓
An amount that has been received in advance from a customer	
An allowance for doubtful debts	
Goods for resale that will be sold next month	
Cash in hand	

Task 3

This task is about preparing financial statements for sole traders.

You have the following trial balance for a sole trader, Tom Kassam. All the necessary year-end adjustments have been made.

(a) **Prepare a statement of profit or loss for the business for the year ended 31 May 20X6.**

Tom Kassam
Trial balance as at 31 May 20X6

	Dr £	Cr £
Accruals		980
Administration expenses	12,060	
Bank	1,730	
Capital		14,000
Closing inventory	14,320	
Depreciation expense	3,880	
Discounts allowed	1,470	
Distribution expenses	25,340	
Drawings	17,790	
Furniture & fittings accumulated depreciation		6,480
Furniture & fittings at cost	24,800	
Prepayments	1,260	
Cost of goods sold	98,500	
Purchases ledger control account		15,940
Sales		201,560
Sales ledger control account	18,450	
VAT		2,970
Wages	22,330	
	241,930	241,930

Tom Kassam
Statement of profit or loss for the year ended 31 May 20X6

	£	£
Sales revenue		
Cost of goods sold		
Gross profit		
Total expenses		
Profit/(loss) for the year		

(b) **Indicate where the VAT balance should be shown in the financial statements. Choose ONE from:**

	✓
Non-current assets	
Current assets	
Current liabilities	✓
Non-current liabilities	

(c) **Which of the following amounts will appear in both the statement of profit or loss and the statement of financial position?**

	✓
Drawings	
Capital	
Opening inventory	
Closing inventory	✓

Task 4

This task is about accounting for partnerships.

You have the following information about a partnership:

The partners are Nigel and Paula.

- Gavin was admitted to the partnership on 1 June 20X7 when he paid £18,500 into the bank account.

- Profit share, effective until 31 May 20X7:

    - Nigel   25%
    - Paula   75%

- Profit share, effective from 1 June 20X7:

    - Nigel   30%
    - Paula   50%
    - Gavin   20%

- Goodwill was valued at £50,000 on 31 May 20X7.

- Goodwill is to be introduced into the partners' capital accounts on 31 May and then eliminated on 1 June.

(a) **Prepare the capital account for Gavin, the new partner, showing clearly the balance carried down as at 1 June 20X7.**

Capital account – Gavin

	£		£

(b) **Identify whether each of the following statements is true or false.**

	True ✓	False ✓
When a partner retires from a partnership, they must always be paid what they are owed in cash.		✓
If the partners agree to change their profit shares, this must take effect from the beginning of the accounting period whatever the partners may agree between themselves.		✓

Task 5

This task is about partnership accounts.

You have the following information about a partnership:

- The financial year ends on 30 September 20X5.

- The partners are William, Richard and Steve.

- Partners' annual salaries:

  - William £15,600
  - Richard £17,200
  - Steve £12,900

- Partners' capital account balances as at 30 September 20X5:

  - William £100,000
  - Richard £80,000
  - Steve £60,000

Interest on capital is charged at 1% per annum on the capital account balance at the end of the financial year.

- The partners share the remaining profit of £72,000 as follows:

  - William 30%
  - Richard 45%
  - Steve 25%

- Partners' drawings for the year:

  - William £22,890
  - Richard £51,250
  - Steve £17,240

Prepare the current accounts for the partners for the year ended 30 September 20X5. Show clearly the balances carried down. You MUST enter zeros where appropriate in order to obtain full marks. Do NOT use brackets, minus signs or dashes.

Current accounts

	William £	Richard £	Steve £		William £	Richard £	Steve £
Balance b/d	0	1,230	950	Balance b/d	200	0	0
	22890	1250	2240		1560	1220	1200
					100	80	60
					2160	3240	1860

BPP PRACTICE ASSESSMENT 2 PREPARE FINAL ACCOUNTS FOR SOLE TRADERS AND PARTNERSHIPS

ANSWERS

Task 1

(a) Purchases ledger control account

		£			£
Bank	▼	60,300	Balance b/d	▼	9,250
Discounts received	▼	4,900	Purchase day-book	▼	67,200
Balance c/d	▼	11,250		▼	
	▼			▼	
		76,450			76,450

(b) VAT control

		£			£
Purchase day-book	▼	11,200	Balance b/d	▼	555
General expenses	▼	210	Sales day-book	▼	17,800
Bank	▼	1,500	Cash sales	▼	200
Sales returns day-book	▼	500		▼	
Balance c/d	▼	5,145		▼	
	▼			▼	
		18,555			18,555

(c) £ | 890 | credit ▼

Task 2

(a)

£	4,000 loss

Workings

	£
Assets 1 January 20X8	20,000
Liabilities 1 January 20X8	14,000
Owner's capital at 1 January 20X8	6,000
	£
Assets 31 December 20X8	30,000
Liabilities 31 December 20X8	20,000
Owner's capital at 31 December 20X8	10,000

Capital account

	£		£
Loss (bal fig)	4,000	Balance b/d	6,000
Balance c/d	10,000	Capital introduced	8,000
	14,000		14,000

(b)

£	59,500

(c)

£	55,360

Workings

	£	%
Sales revenue	95,200	160
Cost of goods sold (95,200 x 100/160)	59,500	100
Gross profit	35,700	60
Opening inventory	22,560	
Purchases (bal fig)	55,360	
Closing inventory	(18,420)	
Cost of goods sold (from above)	59,500	

(d)

Balances	Current asset ✓	Current liability ✓	Neither ✓
Accrual		✓	
Opening inventory			✓
Prepayment	✓		
Loan from bank payable in five years			✓
Bank overdraft		✓	

(e)

	✓
An amount that has been received in advance from a customer	✓
An allowance for doubtful debts	
Goods for resale that will be sold next month	
Cash in hand	

Task 3

(a)

Tom Kassam
Statement of profit or loss for the year ended 31 May 20X6

	£	£
Sales revenue		201,560
Cost of goods sold		(98,500)
Gross profit		103,060
Less:		
Depreciation expense	3,880	
Discounts allowed	1,470	
Distribution expenses	25,340	
Administration expenses	12,060	
Wages	22,330	
Total expenses		(65,080)
Profit for the year		37,980

(b)

	✓
Non-current assets	
Current assets	
Current liabilities	✓
Non-current liabilities	

(c)

	✓
Drawings	
Capital	
Opening inventory	
Closing inventory	✓

Task 4

(a) **Capital account – Gavin**

	£		£
Goodwill	10,000	Balance b/d	0
Balance c/d	8,500	Bank	18,500
	18,500		18,500

(b)

	True ✓	False ✓
When a partner retires from a partnership, they must always be paid what they are owed in cash.		✓
If the partners agree to change their profit shares, this must take effect from the beginning of the accounting period whatever the partners may agree between themselves.		✓

Task 5

Current accounts

	William £	Richard £	Steve £		William £	Richard £	Steve £
Balance b/d	0	1,230	950	Balance b/d	200	0	0
Drawings	22,890	51,250	17,240	Salaries	15,600	17,200	12,900
Balance c/d	15,510	0	13,310	Interest on capital	1,000	800	600
				Profit share	21,600	32,400	18,000
				Balance c/d	0	2,080	0
	38,400	52,480	31,500		38,400	52,480	31,500

BPP PRACTICE ASSESSMENT 3
PREPARE FINAL ACCOUNTS FOR SOLE TRADERS AND PARTNERSHIPS

Time allowed: 2 hours

Task 1

This task is about incomplete records and reconstructing general ledger accounts.

You are working on the financial statements of a business for the year ended 31 March 20X1. The business is not registered for VAT. You have the following information:

	Balance at 31 March 20X0	Balance at 31 March 20X1
Trade receivables	39,000	27,500
Trade payables	15,600	18,950

Discounts allowed during the year amounted to £7,400 and discounts received were £2,610. A contra entry of £830 was made between the sales and purchases ledger control accounts.

Bank account summary

	£		£
Balance b/d	59,150	Sundry expenses	460
Trade receivables	195,240	Trade payables	84,230
Rental income	1,500	Wages	34,780
		Drawings	12,000
		Balance c/d	124,420
	255,890		255,890

(a) **Calculate the figure for sales for the year by preparing the sales ledger control account.**

Sales ledger control account

	£		£
	39000		27500
			830
			7400
			195240

(b) **Calculate the figure for purchases for the year by preparing the purchases ledger control account.**

Purchases ledger control account

	£		£
c/d	18950	b/d	15600
Bank	84230	Purch @	91020
D. Rec	2610		
Cont	830		
	106620		106620

(c) At 1 January 20X5 suppliers were owed £20,000, by 31 December 20X5 they were owed £16,000. In the year, receivables and payables contras were £7,000, and £700 of debit balances were transferred to receivables. Credit purchases were £120,000 and £5,000 of discounts were received.

What was paid to suppliers during the year?

	✓
£111,300	
£112,000	✓
£112,700	
£116,000	

Task 2

(a) This task is about calculating missing balances and the preparation of financial statements.

A business had net assets at the start of the year of £47,390 and at the end of the year of £57,150. The business made a profit of £34,740 for the year.

Use the T account below to calculate the drawings made by the owner in the year.

£	24980

24980

Capital account

	£		£
	57150		47390
	24980		34740

You are given the following information about a shop for one financial year:

Sales for the year amounted to £42,000, the opening inventory was £4,700 and purchases were £30,000. Gross profit margin is 33⅓%.

(b) **Calculate the figure for cost of goods sold.**

£ [   ]

(c) **Calculate the figure for closing inventory.**

£ [3199]

(d) **The proprietor takes goods that had cost the business £250 from the shop for her own personal consumption. Tick the boxes to show the effect of this on the accounts of the business. You must choose ONE answer for EACH line.**

	Debit ✓	Credit ✓	No effect ✓
Bank			(
Drawings	✓		
Inventory			(
Purchases		✓	

(e) **Which of the following statements concerning credit entries is INCORRECT? Choose ONE answer.**

	✓
Credit entries record increases in capital or liabilities	✓
Credit entries record decreases in assets	
Credit entries record increases in profits	
Credit entries record increases in expenses	✓

Task 3

This task is about preparing financial statements for sole traders.

You have the following trial balance for a sole trader, Colin Woodward. All the necessary year-end adjustments have been made.

(a) **Prepare a statement of profit or loss for the business for the year ended 31 March 20X0.**

Colin Woodward
Trial balance as at 31 March 20X0

	Dr £	Cr £
Sales revenue		218,396
Cost of goods sold	79,474	
Discounts allowed	3,260	
Trade receivables and payables	22,863	8,367
Non-current assets at cost	57,150	
Accumulated depreciation		24,840
Motor expenses	1,374	
Wages and salaries	84,381	
Bank balance	2,654	
Rent, rates and insurance	28,012	
General expenses	4,111	
Capital		65,373
Heat and light	12,241	
Closing inventory	13,142	
Deprecation charge	8,314	
	316,976	316,976

Colin Woodward
Statement of profit or loss for the year ended 31 March 20X0

	£	£
Sales revenue		218396
Cost of goods sold		79474
Gross profit		138922
D · A 3260		
M G 1374		
W S 84381		
R 28012		
4 4811		
H M L . 12241		
D P L . 8314		1 ,
Total expenses		
Profit/(loss) for the year Loss		1

(b) **Which of the following best explains the term 'current asset'?**

	✓
An asset currently in use by a business	
Something a business has or uses, likely to be held for only a short time	✓
An amount owed to somebody else which is due for repayment soon	
Money which the business currently has in its bank account	

(c) **Which of the following statements concerning journal entries is correct?**

	✓
Journal entries need not be authorised	
Journal entries are used only to correct errors	✓
The journal is one of the ledgers of the business	
All journal entries must have a narrative explanation	

Task 4

This task is about partnership accounts. Note for students: the two parts of this task use the same names but are independent of each other.

(a) **You have the following information about a partnership business:**

- The financial year ends on 31 March.

- The partners at the beginning of the year were James, Kenzie and Lewis.

- James retired on 30 September 20X0.

- Partners' annual salaries:

  - James   £41,000
  - Kenzie   £50,000
  - Lewis   Nil

- Partners' interest on capital:

  - James   £3,000 per full year
  - Kenzie   £3,000 per full year
  - Lewis   £3,000 per full year

- Profit share, effective until 30 September 20X0:

  - James   60%
  - Kenzie   20%
  - Lewis   20%

- Profit share, effective from 1 October 20X0:

  - Kenzie   75%
  - Lewis   25%

Profit for the year ended 31 March 20X1 was £200,000. You can assume that profits accrued evenly during the year.

Prepare the appropriation account for the partnership for the year ended 31 March 20X1.

Partnership Appropriation account for the year ended 31 March 20X1

	1 April X0 – 30 September X0 £	1 October X0 – 31 March X1 £	Total £
Profit for the year	100 000	100 000	200 000
Salaries:			
James	20 500	—	20 500
Kenzie	25 000	25 000	50 000
Lewis	—	—	
Interest on capital:			
James	1 500	—	1 500
Kenzie	1 500	1 500	3 000
Lewis	1 500	1 500	3 000
Profit available for distribution	50 000	72 000	122 000

Profit share			
James	30 000	—	30 000
Kenzie	10 000	54 000	64 000
Lewis	10 000	18 000	28 000
Total profit distributed	50 000	72 000	122 000

(b) **You have the following different information about the partnership:**

- The financial year ends on 31 March.

- The partners are James, Kenzie and Lewis.

- Partners' annual salaries:
  - James   £16,500
  - Kenzie   £36,000
  - Lewis   nil

- Partners' capital account balances as at 31 March 20X1:
  - James   £50,000
  - Kenzie   £100,000
  - Lewis   £100,000

Interest on capital is charged at 6% per annum on the capital account balance at the end of the financial year.

- The partners share the remaining profit of £80,000 as follows:

  – James 30%
  – Kenzie 50%
  – Lewis 20%

- Partners' drawings for the year:

  – James £32,000
  – Kenzie £80,000
  – Lewis £26,000

Prepare the current accounts for the partners for the year ended 31 March 20X1. Show clearly the balances carried down. You MUST enter zeros where appropriate in order to obtain full marks. Do NOT use brackets, minus signs or dashes.

Current accounts

	James £	Kenzie £	Lewis £		James £	Kenzie £	Lewis £
Balance b/d	800	0	0	Balance b/d	0	3,000	8,600
D	32 000	80000	26000	S	16500	36000	–
	14400	5000	460	Int	200	600	600
	1070			P2	24000	40000	16000
	————	————	————		————	————	————
	═══════	═══════	═══════		43500	85000	30600

Task 5

Partnership statement of financial position

This task is about preparing a partnership statement of financial position.

You are preparing the statement of financial position for the Jasper Partnership for the year ended 31 March 20X1. The partners are Aldo and Billy.

All the necessary year-end adjustments have been made, except for the transfer of profit to the current accounts of the partners.

Before sharing profits the balances of the partners' current accounts are:

- Aldo   £366 credit
- Billy   £600 credit

Each partner is entitled to £7,500 profit share.

(a) **Calculate the balance of each partner's current account after sharing profits. Fill in the answers below.**

Current account balance: Aldo   £ _7866_

Current account balance: Billy   £ _8100_

Note: these balances will need to be transferred into the statement of financial position of the partnership which follows.

You have the following trial balance. All the necessary year-end adjustments have been made.

(b) **Prepare a statement of financial position for the partnership as at 31 March 20X1. You need to use the partners' current account balances that you have just calculated. Do NOT use brackets, minus signs or dashes.**

Jasper Partnership
Trial balance as at 31 March 20X1

	Dr	Cr
	£	£
Accruals		1,190
Administration expenses	39,230	
Bank	4,276	
Capital – Aldo		35,000
Capital – Billy		20,000
Cash	690	
Closing inventory	20,570	20,570
Current account – Aldo		366
Current account – Billy		600
Depreciation charge	4,525	
Disposal of non-current asset	750	
Motor vehicles at cost	43,500	
Motor vehicles accumulated depreciation		12,125
Opening inventory	23,027	
Allowance for doubtful debts		830
Purchases	104,250	
Purchases ledger control account		32,950
Sales		178,785
Sales ledger control account	53,765	
Selling expenses	12,573	
VAT		4,740
Total	307,156	307,156

Jasper Partnership
Trial balance as at 31 March 20X1

	Cost £	Depreciation £	Carrying amount £
Non-current assets	43500	12125	31375
Current assets			
Bank a/c	4966		
C.T.	20530		
D.e.	45847750	79301	
SLCA	53765	80051 —	
		830	
		78471	
Current liabilities			
A c	1190		
PLCA	32950		39571
VAT	4740	38880	
			78966
Net current assets			
Net assets			
Financed by:	Aldo	Billy	Total
Capital	35000	20000	55000
Cur A/c	7866	8100	15966
Profit	7500	7500	15000
Drawn			85966

70966

BPP PRACTICE ASSESSMENT 3
PREPARE FINAL ACCOUNTS FOR SOLE TRADERS AND PARTNERSHIPS

ANSWERS

Task 1

(a) Sales ledger control account

	£		£
Balance b/d	39,000	Bank	195,240
Sales	191,970	Discounts allowed	7,400
		Contra with PLCA	830
		Balance c/d	27,500
	230,970		230,970

(b) Purchases ledger control account

	£		£
Bank	84,230	Balance b/d	15,600
Discounts received	2,610	Purchases	91,020
Contra with SLCA	830		
Balance c/d	18,950		
	106,620		106,620

(c)

	✓
£111,300	
£112,000	
£112,700	✓
£116,000	

Workings

Payables control account

	£		£
Contra	7,000	Balance b/d	20,000
Discounts received	5,000	Transfers to receivables	700
Cash paid (bal fig)	112,700	Purchases	120,000
Balance c/d	16,000		
	140,700		140,700

Task 2

(a)

£	24,980

Workings

Capital account

	£		£
Drawings (bal fig)	24,980	Balance b/d	47,390
Balance c/d	57,150	Profit	34,740
	82,130		82,130

(b)

£	28,000

(c)

£	6,700

Workings

	£	%
Sales revenue	42,000	100
Cost of goods sold	28,000	66⅔
Gross profit	14,000	33⅓
Opening inventory	4,700	
Purchases	30,000	
Closing inventory (balancing figure)	(6,700)	
Cost of goods sold (from above)	28,000	

(d)

	Debit ✓	Credit ✓	No effect ✓
Bank			✓
Drawings	✓		
Inventory			✓
Purchases		✓	

(e)

	✓
Credit entries record increases in capital or liabilities	
Credit entries record decreases in assets	
Credit entries record increases in profits	
Credit entries record increases in expenses	✓

Task 3

(a) **Colin Woodward**
Statement of profit or loss for the year ended 31 March 20X0

	£	£
Sales revenue		218,396
Cost of goods sold		(79,474)
Gross profit		138,922
Less:		
Discounts allowed	3,260	
Motor expenses	1,374	
Heat and light	12,241	
Rent, rates and insurance	28,012	
Wages and salaries	84,381	
General expenses	4,111	
Depreciation	8,314	
Total expenses		(141,693)
Profit/(loss) for the year		(2,771)

(b)

	✓
An asset currently in use by a business	
Something a business has or uses, likely to be held for only a short time	✓
An amount owed to somebody else which is due for repayment soon	
Money which the business currently has in its bank account	

(c)

	✓
Journal entries need not be authorised	
Journal entries are used only to correct errors	
The journal is one of the ledgers of the business	
All journal entries must have a narrative explanation	✓

Task 4

(a) Partnership appropriation account for the year ended 31 March 20X1

	1 April X0 – 30 September X0 £	1 October X0 – 31 March X1 £	Total £
Profit for the year	100,000	100,000	200,000
Salaries:			
James	20,500	0	20,500
Kenzie	25,000	25,000	50,000
Lewis	0	0	0
Interest on capital:			
James	1,500	0	1,500
Kenzie	1,500	1,500	3,000
Lewis	1,500	1,500	3,000
Profit available for distribution	50,000	72,000	122,000

Profit share:			
James	30,000	0	30,000
Kenzie	10,000	54,000	64,000
Lewis	10,000	18,000	28,000
Total profit distributed	50,000	72,000	122,000

(b) Current accounts

	James £	Kenzie £	Lewis £		James £	Kenzie £	Lewis £
Balance b/d	800	0	0	Balance b/d	0	3,000	8,600
Drawings	32,000	80,000	26,000	Salaries	16,500	36,000	0
Balance c/d	10,700	5,000	4,600	Interest on capital	3,000	6,000	6,000
				Profit share	24,000	40,000	16,000
	43,500	85,000	30,600		43,500	85,000	30,600

Task 5

(a)

Aldo	£	7,866 (366 + 7,500)
Billy	£	8,100 (600 + 7,500)

(b) **Jasper Partnership**
Statement of financial position as at 31 March 20X1

	Cost £	Depreciation £	Carrying amount £
Non-current assets			
Motor vehicles at cost	43,500	12,125	31,375
Current assets			
Inventory		20,570	
Trade receivables (53,765 – 830)		52,935	
Bank		4,276	
Cash		690	
		78,471	

	Cost £	Depreciation £	Carrying amount £
Current liabilities			
Trade payables	32,950		
VAT	4,740		
Accruals	1,190		
		38,880	
Net current assets			39,591
Net assets			70,966
Financed by:	Aldo	Billy	Total
Capital accounts	35,000	20,000	55,000
Current accounts	7,866	8,100	15,966
	42,866	28,100	70,966

Notes

Notes

Notes

Notes

Notes

Notes